D0829174

Praise for Raising Humans With Heart

If you've parented for longer than two months, you're probably craving a parenting book that is vivid, to-the-point, and written by someone who can frankly admit how hard parenting can be. Raising Humans With Heart is that book. In it, you'll find wisdom and humility, brevity and clarity, and some memorable parenting stories. It has the recipe for raising sound children in today's world, and a warmth that will bring you back to it again and again.

–Patty Wipfler, founder of Hand in Hand Parenting and coauthor of Listen

This is a parenting book for the ages. In this succinct and well-articulated book, Sarah MacLaughlin shares her wisdom with grace and clarity. She touches on a myriad of parenting essentials—brain development, empathy, gratitude and the vital importance of self-awareness—to guide parents inward toward knowing and trusting themselves and their growing people. As she says, "it's not a how-to manual" but it is definitely guidance on ways of being with ourselves and our growing people. What a gift!

–Carrie Contey, PhD, author of CALMS: A guide to soothing your baby

In her new book, Raising Humans With Heart, Sarah MacLaughlin shows up as the friend every parent needs. She reminds us that the journey is messy, while also encouraging us to embrace the process.

–Casey O'Roarty, M.Ed., Positive Discipline Trainer, author, and host of the Joyful Courage Parenting Podcast

Raising Humans With Heart provides a missing roadmap for parents to help them model emotional intelligence for their children. This book is really about the art of being a human being...for parents as well as their children. This practical, tangible, down-to-earth guide helps parents grow emotionally literate, well-balanced, kind, and functional adults. Sarah MacLaughlin is a knowledgeable girlfriend offering well-worn tips over a hot cup of tea on a rainy afternoon. Every page is filled with kindness and compassion for the challenging task of being a parent. I agree with Sarah when she says, "I believe we can transform the future by adjusting how we raise children."

–Tina M. Benson, M.A., author of A Woman Unto Herself: A Different Kind of Love Story

In Raising Humans With Heart, Sarah MacLaughlin reminds us that who and how we are matters more than what we do. Filled with deep wisdom, valuable insights, and personal stories, this book is a joy to read! Sarah's forward-thinking message goes straight to the heart. If you want to raise compassionate, caring, and brave children who will shift the trajectory of humankind, you need to parent from the heart. Given the times we live in, this book is an essential guidebook. Bold, progressive, and brilliant.

–Anna Seewald, MEd, host of the Authentic Parenting podcast

Raising Humans With Heart is precisely the kind of book we need more of in the world right now. Sarah MacLaughlin's uncanny ability to blend sage parenting wisdom, relatable stories, relevant neuroscience, and thoughtfully curated resources makes for an inspiring and practical guide parents can put into practice immediately. This gentle, beautifully written book offers a deeper inquiry into what it takes to raise humans in a more empathic, just, and compassionate world.

–Shelly Robinson, founder of Raising Yourself

Raising Humans With Heart makes space for respectful parenting to be both accessible and sustainable within the constraints of modern parenthood. Sarah looks at what it means to be fully human, for both children and adults, and how to navigate raising kids and reparenting ourselves with connection, collaboration, and joy.

–Alyssa Blask Campbell, M.Ed., founder of Seed & Sew and host of the Voices of Your Village podcast

Raising Humans With Heart is a great tool to begin to implement practices in parenting that lead to more liberated young people. In a world full of oppression and domination, we must be intentional to not reproduce these harms within our interpersonal relationships. Sarah's work gives those committed to the work of transforming, a place to start with thoughtfulness, curiosity, and compassion.

–Jasmine Banks, cofounder of Parenting is Political and mom of 4

This book is not only timely, it's actually timeless. Helping parents understand how to connect with their children during the highs and lows of life is a topic that can be utilized over and over again. We must all learn to raise kind and whole humans by being kind and whole humans ourselves. Sarah's newest addition to this conversation is exactly what we need in a time where connection, kindness, empathy, and healthy emotional development are much needed.

–Mercedes Samudio, LCSW, author of Shameproof Parenting: Find your unique parenting voice, feel empowered, and raise whole, healthy children

Reading this book feels as though you're spending an evening with your best friend, who makes you a cup of tea and hands you a warm blanket as all your biggest fears about raising resilient kids in an unpredictable world spill out. Each chapter eases your mind with a comforting story about the joys of being imperfectly human and honoring the small steps children make along the road to maturity.

–Lori Petro, Child Advocate and creator of the Teach Through Love Conscious Communication Cards

This book will have you nodding your head emphatically, bursting into laughter, and welling up with tears—sometimes all on the same page. In her straightforward way, Sarah has brilliantly brought

science and heart to the page to share what kids need most in order to have the best possible shot at this thing called life. Read this book and feel inspired and empowered to know that you have got this!

–Dr. Vanessa Lapointe, author of Discipline Without Damage and the forthcoming Parenting Right From the Start. Dr. Vanessa is a registered psychologist, parenting educator, and mom

Sarah MacLaughlin's Raising Humans With Heart is a book with heart. Blending stories with science and our "superpowers" inherent in relationships, Sarah guides us with love and leadership to reclaim our deepest purpose in raising children to thrive in the world. Courage comes from coeur meaning heart. Sarah reminds us that when we draw from our deepest courage in the face of our fears, we parent with heart to raise kids who know their own hearts too.

–Lu Hanessian, MSc, award-winning writer, author of the acclaimed book Let the Baby Drive: Navigating the Road of the New Motherhood, The Garden: A Parenting Parable, and the forthcoming book Return to Tender. Lu is an educator, resilience researcher, and consultant, founder of Raising the Future Now, former NBC Network anchor, and host of Make Room for Baby on the Discovery Health Channel

Sarah's years of training, experience, and whole-hearted compassion shine through on each page as she masterfully weaves insight and personal stories together in an informative and empowering way. A must-have book for anyone who loves children.

–Bridgett Miller, author of What Young Children Need You to Know: How to see them so you know what to do for them

Raising Humans With Heart is a lovely read that normalizes the emotions that come with parenting and is full of care and compassion for kids and the adults who raise them.

–Deborah MacNamara, PhD, author of Rest, Play, Grow: Making Sense of Preschoolers (or anyone who acts like one)

This may not be a how-to manual, but you will be gently moved to infuse more moments with gratitude, playfulness, listening, boundaries, self-compassion—and get the close relationship you really want.

–Tracy Cutchlow, author of international bestseller Zero to Five: 70 Essential Parenting Tips Based on Science

As a millennial, late-bloomer, parent-to-be, this book helps subside the fears we all have about raising kids, and gives us REAL examples of how NOT to mess them up...I will happily force my husband to read this!

–Audrey Brazeel, author of Generation Nanny

Sarah MacLaughlin writes a funny, humble, and honest account of the stamina and vulnerability required to raise humans with heart. Sharing real life stories, she talks about why setting limits is important while also acknowledging how difficult it can be. She notes that limits are a necessary ebb and flow, and that this fluidity, rather than indicating "poor parenting," actually mirrors the flexibility necessary for life. Sarah discusses topics from brain science and responding to challenging behaviors, to the importance of witnessing our children's pain as a form of building resilience and emotional capacity. She teaches us to amplify joy in our lives, pull our expectations out of the clouds and back into reality, and encourages us to really look at the ways we are with our children daily. Sarah speaks from a place of experience, education, and compassion. Her book is an invitation to breathe a deep sigh of relief and a simultaneous call to compassionate action: you are not alone, you are not a failure, here are some ways to increase your ability to model healthy, relationship, and science-centered lessons on life, love, and being human.

–Amy C. Bryant, EdS, LPC, founder of Wild Child Counseling & Parenting Beyond Punishment

This book explains, in a meaningful way, how our own emotional intelligence is reflected in our parenting. It can help parents to understand why they feel and react the way they do sometimes.

–J. Milburn, Responsive Parenting Mentor and Child Development Specialist

This book has everything I want in a parenting book—honesty, humility, and empathy combined with practical advice and chock-full of real-life stories and examples. Sarah shares her heart—and her most heartfelt advice. A must-read for parents at all stages of parenthood.

–Katherine Endy, The Family Life Coach

Desmond Tutu said, "There comes a point where we need to stop just pulling people out of the river. We need to go upstream and find out why they're falling in." If parenting is the proverbial journey along the river, Sarah has climbed upstream, studied the river, listened to the people, and found out why they're falling in. In these pages we are reminded of how to harness the river's energy for good, to work with the ebb and flow, keep it clean, build secure bridges, and learn how to swim. It makes sense to be occasionally daunted and other times delighted on the journey. As we listen to the heart and safely guide our children to listen to theirs, we can walk bravely alongside the river, dipping in and out when wanted or needed. Raising Humans With Heart is rich in resources based on the latest neuroscience and overflowing with eternal heart-wisdom. The messages have the power to gently ignite and affirm parents' innate intuition. Words like seeds which will grow deep roots and blossoming branches if nurtured by the reader. This work is activism, but I too dream of a world where raising humans with heart will be deeply known and naturally lived by our children, and our children's children's children...

–Lelia Schott, founder of Synergy: gentle parenting

Life during the Covid-19 pandemic has left me feeling dull, exhausted, and uninspired. Quarantine and long days at home have given me many "growing opportunities" when it comes to parenting my three children. I have been hesitant to pick up any books about parenting, because the LAST thing I need is someone telling me I am not doing things "right" during this time of crisis. However, I am SO glad I had the opportunity to read and savor this beautiful, and incredibly practical book. Raising Humans With Heart has given me real, accessible parenting tools and allowed me to step outside of patterned perception. As a result, I have a fresh perspective on parenting along with a host of accessible and meaningful ways to connect with my children. I can see their inherent goodness again, as well as my own, and I could not be more grateful for this much needed shift. Thank you, Sarah!

–Reverend Sarah L. Siegel, Interfaith Minister, Writer, and Mindfulness, Meditation, and Recovery Coach

Raising Humans With Heart is a wonderfully accessible read. A gentle road map that shuns old authority, "rewards and punishment" style thinking, and really champions the importance of good, authentic relationships, community, and self-care. It's a warm, wise, and hopeful book, peppered with anecdotes and plenty of pointers to further reading, in case you'd like to dive a little deeper.

–NVRnorthampton

Raising Humans With Heart brings an imagined future where "children are honored and parents are supported" into the present through deeply compassionate insights and well-researched neuroscience. MacLaughlin's clear, concise guidance can help you exchange the disconnected, cultural fantasy of parenting for the connected, joyful relationships that build lifelong resiliency. This book borders on poetry, every page a heart-opening revelation to nurture you and your children.

–Lisa Reagan, founder of Kindred World and Editor of Kindred Media

Raising Humans With Heart is a love letter to life itself, addressed to all parents and caregivers, and so very pertinent in today's ever-changing and unpredictable world. Looking for a guide that gently steers you in the right direction that is founded in brain science? Well look no further! Sarah MacLaughlin has outdone herself with simple down-to-earth examples of how we can update and edit our own often dusty parenting manuals. She offers us the important reminder that as older humans who have been here longer, it is our responsibility to usher our children with respect, love, and compassion. This book will help you reduce the stress you might feel around children of all ages (remember humans have the longest childhood at 20+ years), and will help you create a peaceful home and strong connected relationships with your confident offspring.

–Jeanne-Marie Paynel, M.Ed.,
host of The Art of Parenting podcast

In Raising Humans With Heart, Sarah MacLaughlin gifts us with an invaluable resource: stories about actual interactions with her son when he was being especially challenging, and her own words and actions in response. These vignettes demonstrate how any parent, even when angry, can almost magically transform a tough situation with their child—IF they can resist coercion.

-Dr. Laura Markham, author of
Peaceful Parent, Happy Kids
and founder of Aha! Parenting

While there is no such thing as a parenting manual that fits every child, there is much wisdom we can glean from educators and moms who have gone before us. This book is filled with that wisdom. Sarah makes it digestible in this must-have addition to your parenting repertoire.

-Rebecca Eanes, author of
Positive Parenting: An Essential Guide
and *The Gift of a Happy Mother*

RAISING HUMANS WITH HEART

Also by Sarah MacLaughlin

What Not to Say: Tools for Talking with Young Children

RAISING HUMANS WITH HEART

Not a How-To Manual

SARAH MACLAUGHLIN

Isabella Media Inc

Raising Humans With Heart
Not a How-To Manual
Published by Isabella Media Inc.
Text Copyright by Sarah MacLaughlin
270 Bellevue Ave #1002,
Newport RI 02840
www.IsabellaMedia.com

© 2020 Isabella Media Inc.

All rights reserved. No portion of this book may be reproduced in any form without permission from the publisher, except as permitted by U.S. copyright law.

ISBN-13: 978-1-7357256-2-8

For permissions contact: requests@isabellamedia.com

"It's not our job to toughen our children up to face a cruel and heartless world. It's our job to raise children who will make the world a little less cruel and heartless."

–L.R. Knost

CONTENTS

FOREWORD

Hello, I'm Pam Leo, author of the book, *Connection Parenting*, best known for the quote, "Let's raise children who won't have to recover from their childhoods." I'm also a literacy activist and the founder of the international grassroots children's literacy movement, the Book Fairy Pantry Project.

Sarah MacLaughlin is my friend and much respected colleague. We have known each other for at least 12 years as her son and my grandson both turn 12 this year, and they have been best buds since they were babies. I have the unique perspective of knowing Sarah both personally and professionally. Sometimes I see her at my daughter's home in her role as "mom," and sometimes, we rideshare to professional development conferences when we are both presenting parenting workshops.

"My best friend is a person who will give me a book I have not read."
–Abraham Lincoln

I rarely attempt to give Sarah a parenting book as a gift, even though it is her favorite reading topic. Why? Because it is too difficult to find one she hasn't read. I have read more parenting books than most, but Sarah has read more parenting books than any parent I know. She devours them like she does my special popcorn. What parent has the time and the motivation to read so many parenting books? It would have to be one whose profession requires them to spend many hours researching and writing about parenting, or one who is driven to learn all she could about the best ways to nurture her own child. For Sarah it is both.

I recently spent some time with her son and my grandson, our two "boyos," as we so fondly call them. During that time, I realized that Sarah's son Josh is the best evidence I can point to that the kind of parenting she writes about here has great merit. Is he a perfect child? Heck no. He is human like all our children. But, if the definition of a "human with heart" is a loving, respectful, considerate, caring, compassionate, generous, funny, affectionate, intelligent young person, then I must say...bravo! Sarah and Rich—so far so good.

The gift I see in Sarah's book, to quote her words, is a "new lens" through which to see the job of parenting. She shares with us the best of what she has learned from the writings of some of the greatest minds who have explored human development and behavior. To that solid academic foundation, Sarah adds her 20 plus years of experience working directly with families, and finally her 12 years of pursuing the art of nurturing a growing human being.

I told Sarah she is a "cream separator." For those who did not spend time at their Grampie's small, north-country dairy farm in the 1950s, a cream separator is a metal dairy device with a paper disc filter, two spouts, and a crank handle. My Grampie would pour the fresh, raw milk into the separator, then I got to turn the crank handle and watch with wonder as the milk came out one spout and the cream came out the other. That sweet cream gave me yet another opportunity to turn a crank, as I helped my Grammie churn that cream into butter.

It takes four gallons of milk to get the half gallon of cream needed to make one pound of butter. I declare this book to be...parenting butter. What it took Sarah years to gather, skim, and churn, we get to read in one book. If you are looking for a book with information on how to control your children's behavior, it would be best to put this one back and keep looking. If, however, you are looking for a book that will teach you many ways of being with children that will support you in creating a close, loving connection with them, read on.

"Our parenting is not decided in moments of failure, but in the ways we choose to learn from those failures and change our future responses." -Dr. David Erickson

If I had parenting to do over again, would I do everything exactly like Sarah does? No, that would be silly. Since no two parents are alike, and no two children are alike, that would never work. But what is required to create and maintain connection is always the same. When parents begin seeing the job of parenting through the new lens of connection, and learn what Sarah has learned and shared, they will have the tools to create the conditions for *raising humans with heart.*

Pam Leo
Author, *Connection Parenting*
Founder, Book Fairy Pantry Project
Portland, Maine
August 2020

WHAT IS THIS BOOK, AND WHY READ IT?

"I don't think anyone can grow unless he's loved exactly as he is now, appreciated for what he is rather than what he will be." –Fred Rogers

What is a "good" life?

When I began writing this book, a friend sent me this message: *I'm counting on a full explanation of how to live life! I feel like parenting is getting more existential as we get closer to adolescence.* I agreed and she elaborated about her experience parenting her daughter. She wrote: *I feel like I want to help her develop a toolkit of skills and experiences for a good life, but I'm not sure what a good life is.*

That got me thinking, *What IS a good life?* And what's the answer? That depends on so much. Who you are. What your values are. What community environment or subculture you grew up in. Not to mention race, ethnicity, and religion. There are so many factors.

My thoughts on a good life, and herein on "good" parenting, are all seen through my own lens as a white, cis, straight, middle-aged, middle-class woman. Of course, these labels are always so incomplete. For a little added nuance: I was raised by working-class hippies, am more of a 1.5 on the Kinsey scale, and am of Jewish descent. But for all intents and purposes, the labels stand. So keep that in mind as you read. Because my perspective and beliefs, like yours, have been shaped by my background and experiences. We all have biases and we can't address them if we don't even see them. In the last chapter of this book I will dive into the importance of raising children in an anti-bias manner and with an antiracist, feminist, anti-homophobic lens.

I have written this book with typically developing children from toddlers to teens in mind, as that's where my expertise lies. I hope it can be useful for any parent, teacher, or caregiver, and also for those who are reparenting themselves. I encourage you to read with curiosity and take what fits and leave what doesn't. As always, you know your own children and family best.

One thing I think makes a good life is *having heart*. Having heart might mean wearing yours on your sleeve. It might mean letting it break. It might mean staying open in the face of difficulty. It takes perspective-shifting and deep listening to dig into what it means to have heart, and to raise children with yours open so theirs can be open too. I don't know about you, but I spend *a lot* of time in my head, and getting centered in my heart and being in touch with my body (oh yeah, I have a body!) always seems to help.

I know I'm in my heart when I don't feel in a hurry and have the mental space to *pause*. When I speed up, I'm often on autopilot. Part of what I mean by "heart" is being awake—conscious and attentive to the present moment. This is a state of being I cultivate with a daily meditation practice, but I'm sure there are other ways. The self-nurturing practices that make you feel alive and well-cared for may be different from mine. Part of being a good parent is doing these things so you feel well enough to take care of others. Find the things that help *you* feel this way and make them a priority. Ironically, it seems that another indicator of *doing it right*—life, parenting—is in simply asking the question. It's a paradox that only in making this query do you get at all close to having an answer. The upshot is if you're concerned about getting parenting right, you're probably well on your way to doing so.

All about babies and getting it "right"

My obsession with parenting began as a fascination with babies. From the time I was old enough to hold one, I *loved* babies. I was captivated by their gummy, drooly smiles and their innocent wide-eyed stares. So obviously I babysat more than most. As I grew up and tried to make sense of the world, I kept coming back to babies. They were a touchstone. When I heard the many atrocities that humans have inflicted on each other, I'd think, *But those people used to be babies!* And I knew that all babies were born good. The only explanation I could come up with was that something must have gone terribly wrong after they were born. It's the nurture/nature debate. I thought, *If we only have control over nurture (parenting!), then I want to learn as much as possible about* that.

Decades later, we still haven't figured out what kind of parenting leads to *optimal* human development, but we're getting closer and know that connection and attachment are key. Research also tells us that a harsh, punitive approach is unhelpful and that corporal punishment is damaging. Many parents bounce between permissive parenting (too soft) and authoritarian parenting (too hard), but the sweet, Goldilocks spot is the middleground with the funny name. *Authoritative* parenting is the style that combines high expectations with a sensitive, responsive approach. It's both firm *and* kind.

The other thing that fueled my desire to promote good parenting was *my* upbringing (worthy of its own book, I'm sure). Like most people, I was a recipient of imperfect parenting. My parents did not have the benefit of child development experts, cutting edge brain science, or even really any parenting books. I'm pretty sure my mom had Dr. Spock and that's it.

I had my share of chaos and Adverse Childhood Experiences, but I also had plenty of laughter and fun. My parents did some things really well and in other ways they totally blew it. But they also made me want to learn how to do it better. We will all fail and succeed, but that doesn't mean we shouldn't try to get it right as often as we can.

What if we didn't have to recover?

The quote at the front of my first book, *What Not to Say: Tools for Talking with Young Children,* is author and literacy activist Pam Leo's home-hitting statement: "Let's raise children who don't have to recover from their childhoods." It strikes a chord, doesn't it? Why do so many of us feel we have to recover from the parenting we received? Maybe some things could change?

The old story tells us that we must teach children to behave well through control and coercion. It's common to use punishments and rewards—imposed consequences or loss of privileges for bad behavior—and kudos, treats, and praise for good behavior. Author and parent educator Alfie Kohn's work points out that rewards and punishments are merely opposite sides of the same coin. While these approaches may modify some children's behavior, they also come at a cost. Children who watch us use coercion in our parenting learn from that example. They are always watching us and what *we* do.

Author and former professor Jeree Pawl once said, "How you are is as important as what you do." (She also co-wrote a book with that title.) We don't need to *instruct* our children on how to behave, because we are always *showing* them with our own behavior. We guide our children with *who we are.* I am encouraged to see many other advocates for this shift in parenting (see resource suggestions throughout this book). We *can* move from a place of coercion to one of collaboration, and many have. Or at least we try, it's often a work in progress.

Part of the evolution of parenting is access to amazing brain research. Scientific findings about how babies develop, and how children grow and learn are fascinating additions to general theories of parenting. We can move from a controlling, authority-based, behavioral approach to a cooperative, relationship-based one. If you picked up this book, you might already *want* to parent in this way, but maybe you struggle with a flaring temper of your own or an inability to set both firm and kind limits.

While my intention is for this book to focus on *who and how we are* as parents, and to not be a "how-to," I will share some approaches

Four brain science-based books to help you parent well:
- *Brain Rules for Baby* by John Medina
- *Zero to Five* by Tracy Cutchlow
- *The Whole Brain Child* by Daniel J. Siegel M.D. and Tina Payne Bryson Ph.D.
- *Rest, Play, Grow* by Deborah MacNamara, Ph.D.

and tangible tools that might help you become the parent you want to be. I know it's a paradox, giving advice on parenting while trying not to tell you what to do. I am trained in multiple parenting curricula and dedicate Chapter 5 to sharing about Hand in Hand Parenting's Listening Tools. Besides that, I don't go too far into techniques or even very much theory—there are different books for that, many of them suggested throughout.

I do my best to share my own experiences and stories, and my son's, with his permission. I aim to tell you about the times I embodied the qualities and habits I want my child to have—even when I didn't get it right the first time. Chapter 8 is all about modeling because as much as we'd love the opposite to be true, children always do what we *do* over what we *say*. It doesn't work to merely *tell them* to be understanding, compassionate, curious, hardworking, and kind. If we are not, they likely won't be either.

I promise that raising children without rewards, punishments, and shame is possible. I've been practicing on other people's children for over 25 years, and my own is almost a teenager now. Coercion is not necessary, and in all its forms it hampers positive, connected relationships. I agree with Albert Einstein who once said, "If people are good only because they fear punishment, and hope for reward, then we are a sorry lot indeed."

It's all about community

In our broader world, change is slow going, but we'll get there. It's worth the effort because growing people deserve positive parenting. When children are treated with dignity and respect they grow up to be kind humans. They need a sense of belonging and to feel connected and loved. We guide them well when we balance nurture and structure. Parents can best offer this to their children when they have support. There will still be conflict, but it can be resolved in compassionate ways. Other adults who care about and care for our kids are key. Shout out to alloparents: the aunts, uncles, and other adults who care about and for our kids.

To paraphrase Genevieve Simperingham, founder and director of the Peaceful Parent Institute: We can approach conflict with the understanding that it is happening *because someone is upset*. From this place of emotional sensitivity and awareness, we can slow things down, check in with all parties, and negotiate a solution. We can trust every child's inherent goodness. Our difficulties can be resolved through honest, authentic, and considerate sharing of feelings and problem-solving. If we can work through our own emotions in these moments and try to sort things out together, then we'll have succeeded.

Hope for the future

When I take this line of thinking further, I imagine that one day children will be honored, and parents will be supported. No one will label behavior "bad," or insist that children be "taught a lesson." Parental leave will be standard and parenting education plentiful. Lack of resources for families will be outdated.

In my imagination, I hear someone talking:

"Remember when people didn't respect children or realize they needed to be listened to? Remember spanking and time-outs? Remember when people lost their jobs if they didn't go back to work when their children were tiny? Wasn't that insane?"

We can *and will* shift the trajectory of humankind through kind and loving parenting. It's already happening and it significantly changes the way children's brains grow. These brains, wired through connection and with emotional awareness, will create a different world. I hope you enjoy this information and these encouraging messages and are inspired to join me in creating a new future.

CHAPTER 1

You Already Own a Parenting Manual

"If you ever find yourself in the wrong story, leave." –Mo Willems

One day it dawned on me that about half of my parenting was acting out the beliefs I had inherited from my childhood. The other half was me pushing back *against* those beliefs—trying to avoid the perceived pitfalls of the parenting that I had received. Maybe it would balance out? Maybe my husband was doing the same based on his upbringing?

We all come to parenting with a full (but subconscious) set of instructions gleaned from the way *we* were raised. The problem is, we end up parenting reactively, and from an outdated manual. If you're like most, your manual is a mixed bag. Some things you'll want to keep, others, you'll let go. What's *most* important is knowing that you have this "book" and reviewing it with a critical eye so you can modify your beliefs and rewrite the undesirable sections.

What about motivation?

Most of us grew up with some version of rewards and punishments as motivators. We heard the following refrains:

"Do what you're told."
"Don't talk back."
"Because I said so."

> "That's what Momma said. You are always on the same page!" (When trying for a different answer from Dadda). -Ziggy, 9 years old

Many parents today are grappling with a slightly different problem. We understand that the "my way or the highway" authoritarian approach, while perhaps effective at gaining compliance, is not beneficial to the parent-child relationship. But parents still end up in power struggles over many issues. As a parenting coach, I hear:

"He's always grabbing for power."

"She wants to control everything."

"Don't I have to show them who's boss?"

Our culture doesn't help with its unrealistic expectations and tendency to judge how well a parent parents, by how well a child behaves. Parents are told clearly and often that they should be *in control* of their child's behavior. This is how most of us were raised, but this framework is unhelpful and causes stress for everyone. In truth, the only person whose behavior we can control is *our own*. That's a bitter pill to swallow during the most intensive years of parenting.

I don't know about you, but when I feel powerless, I get panicky and freaked out. When I'm emotional, I'm ineffective as a parent and need to do something to remind myself I still have power. I can always choose to slow down, take a breath or two, and regain some calm. It's hard to remember when you are the adult in the adult-child scenario that *you're* the one with most of the power. Sometimes it feels quite the opposite. While there are many things we can't control, we can always take charge of our behavior and narrative.

That's right, the narrative. Sometimes you need to tell yourself a new story. The stories we tell ourselves are compelling and we tend to believe them. They provide

Three books to help you shift the stories you tell yourself:

- *Daring Greatly* by Brené Brown Ph.D.
- *You Are a Badass* by Jen Sincero
- *The Subtle Art of Not Giving a F*ck* by Mark Manson

context, motivation, and can profoundly affect our behavior. However, that doesn't mean they're always true.

I was recently feeling powerless, with a layer of anger on top, about my child's behavior. Ironically, I desperately wanted him to change his attitude (and story!) about something that had not gone his way, but instead of bringing the calm, I was escalating the stress. *I couldn't do what I wanted *him* to be able to do!* I immediately felt better when I modified my internal story. I started out with, *My kid is terrible, driving me crazy, and I don't deserve this.* Then I shifted to, *This has been a rough day and no one can self-regulate, but this too shall pass.*

When I'm losing my cool and worried that my kid is *the worst*, it helps to remind myself that no matter how "badly" he's behaving, he doesn't deserve to be treated poorly, yelled at, or punished. Those avenues are always counterproductive.

Isn't fear a good motivator?

In a word: No.

I don't want to discount fear. It's essential; primitive, biological, and extremely useful, but not necessarily a great parenting tool. Fear is sometimes needed for survival, but—here's the kicker—not usually. The fear response in our brains, the physical structures and chemical reactions, are very, very old. Author and safety expert, Gavin de Becker, in his national bestseller, *The Gift of Fear*, says that true fear is a gift, an intuitive message that should *always* be heeded. On the flip side, he calls unwarranted fear and worry a curse—it just doesn't serve us. A lot of the fear we feel as parents falls into the worry category, though some is gut panic.

We get scared for any number of reasons. A couple of examples: your two-year-old runs into the street, or your four-year-old throws a tantrum of shocking vileness and force. When either of these things happens, I promise you are *no longer thinking well*. Also, you are *no longer in the present time*.

Step one is to recognize this. When the fear-driven part of your brain, the amygdala, hijacks the thinking part, the prefrontal cortex, and floods your body with adrenaline and cortisol, you are no longer a rational human. You are in either fight, flight, or freeze mode. This is your brain's way of protecting you from danger, but I'm guessing we can agree it's not the best place from which to parent. When your ability to think is literally bypassed, your perception of things gets skewed as this part of your brain sends you into emergency management mode. Things feel more intense because your brain is shouting the message that you're being threatened. This dive into the lower parts of the brain is sometimes called "flipping your lid."

Three TED Talks on brain development and motivation:
- *Wiring the brain for success* by Becky Bailey, Ph.D.
- *How childhood trauma affects health across the lifetime* by Nadine Burke Harris, M.D.
- *The puzzle of motivation* by Dan Pink

Step two is to breathe. When you breathe, you reconnect to yourself and your body in the present moment. When you snatch your child from a busy street, you still imagine them injured or dead, *even though that didn't happen.* You have projected yourself into an imaginary future. And sure, that tantrum was awful, but your preschooler didn't mean those terrible things he said. These are tricks a fearful mind plays—an old response to a new situation. In our modern world, safety is usually restored very quickly. There is no *actual* need to fight, run, or play dead, despite what your body is telling you. Breathing will slow things down and help remind you that *you are safe.*

Step three is to not perpetuate the fear. This is where we often *use* fear as parents. We swat the child who darted into the road, hoping that pain will scare them into never doing it again. We yell at the four-year-old to pull it together, or we separate them in a time-out to "think about" their behavior. Both yelling and time-out are fear-based punishments—the former creates fear through a parent's anger, violence, and pain, and the latter brings fear of the withdrawal of a parent's attention, closeness, and love. A large body of research concludes that physical discipline is never appropriate for children. With regard to time-out, I can see the wisdom of a short break to catch your breath, or its use as a form of harm reduction. But many children who have lost control of their emotions and behavior will regulate *much* more quickly and efficiently with a calm adult near them, rather than being sent away and isolated. Even children who "need space" to settle down, typically want to reconnect once they're calm. Punitive, timed, or forced isolation doesn't allow for this.

All punishments are based in fear, and often consequences are just thinly veiled punishments. I once discussed this with a nice gentleman. I'll call him Joe. In his efforts to convince me of the necessity of enforced consequences, he inquired about my driving habits. He noted that I likely drove the speed limit because of the risk of receiving a ticket (consequence).

Here's what I told Joe: I do *not* drive crazy fast, not because I could get a ticket, but because I've learned it's dangerous and stupid. Do I ever speed? Yes, I often drive five or so miles over the speed limit. Sometimes out of absent-mindedness, sometimes because I'm running late. The possibility of receiving a ticket does not deter me from this type of speeding, but if I see a police officer along the way, I slow down. That's because *the enforcer of the consequence is near.* In this same way, children who are taught to obey out of fear of authority will abide by the rules, *but only when the authority figure is present.*

I'm not sure my argument convinced Joe, but I'm hoping you see my point. Don't we want children to be internally motivated to behave well, to *understand* why they are being guided to behave in certain ways and not in others? Children who are motivated by fear, obey because of it. They learn to be sneaky to avoid punishment. With fear, the true goal of discipline—to teach—is completely lost.

Healthy risk-taking and natural consequences

Three books to help you raise an adult:

- *How to Raise an Adult* by Julie Lythcott-Haims
- *Brainstorm* by Daniel J. Siegel, M.D.
- *The Romance of Risk* by Lynn E. Ponton, M.D.

When children engage in healthy risk-taking, they learn their own limits. This is especially important when I remember I am ultimately raising an adult, not a child. Allowing for this kind of learning doesn't mean we should let them fall on their faces and "grow from the experience." Children *can* learn from some natural consequences safely, but the messages we send *as they experience* those consequences vary widely, as does their impact.

It feels different to stumble, fall, or fail and have your parent say:

"That was a tough one."

"I'm sorry you're going through this," or,

"You're not alone, I'm right here with you."

As opposed to:

"I told you that would happen."

"You just had to learn the hard way," or,

"That'll teach you!"

When embarrassment, failure, or poor judgment are *shamed*, we stop putting ourselves out there. We shrink and play small. We stay inside our comfort zones. Try teaching something else. Offer your growing people support, kindness, guidance, and empathy. Model understanding, generosity, and love.

It comes down to power

In a teacher training years ago, I learned about two types of power: *power-to* and *power-over*. Power-to is our ability to take action and do things for ourselves, while power-over is trying to control others and circumstances outside ourselves. Our goal as parents, teachers, and other caregivers is to promote the former and diminish the latter. The only time an adult person needs to exert power-over a young person is for safety concerns. It's worth noting that children whose power-to gets regularly thwarted will seek to gain power-over with their siblings and peers.

I get calls from parents who want help with providing discipline (in my book it's always a noun, not a verb or something you "do to" a child), handling tantrums, and navigating big feelings—theirs and their children's—with relative grace and good humor. All these issues are rooted in power, specifically, *who has it?* These struggles boil down to the question of who has power *over* whom. *Power-over* is the real problem. When we try to control another person's behavior or emotions (*especially* emotions), we overstep our bounds.

Author and early childhood educator Janet Gonzalez-Mena once said, "Instead of assuming a power stance, a parent can become a problem-solving facilitator." To which I say: Yes! But this is only possible when we step back from the comforting habit of taking over and giving orders.

Our culture reinforces the notion that children need to be tamed, controlled, and socialized, so watch for these thoughts and beliefs. When you catch them, you can rewrite the scripts that guide you in *your* behavior. A few trajectory-altering ideas to get you thinking:

Feeling powerless is no fun. When we don't get what we want—at age four or 40—it's upsetting. I can't overstate how important and helpful it is to make room for this upset. It's the parent's job to *set the limit*. It's the child's job to *feel their feelings about the limit*. Being with a child's feelings often leaves *us* feeling powerless, so we try to shut them down. This is how the cycle continues. However, as parents and caregivers we have a unique opportunity to break this cycle with our behavior. There is nothing inherently *wrong* with big or uncomfortable feelings, other than the fact that most adults were conditioned in early childhood to resist and avoid them.

Power is necessary. When your child is "power-grabbing," they are letting you know they need guidance and support, or a listening ear and a problem-solving coach. If you get triggered, try calming yourself first. Then you'll be able to help regulate the emotional state of your child *along with them*.

Messages about power "stick." When we tell children what to do all the time, or curtail their emotional expression, or use punishment and punitive consequences (or threats, bribes, and our own worries and anxieties) to manage their behavior, we undermine their sense of *power-to* and send the message that they "can't." Think about something you want to do that you haven't been able to accomplish. Is there a tiny voice in your head saying, "I can't"? That voice was wired in, through some experience you had. It did not come from nowhere. Through awareness and neuroplasticity (your brain's ongoing ability to grow), you can alter that little voice. But why not help kids wire healthier self-talk from the start?

The more respectful we can be as adults, even when we need to take charge with growing people, the better. Next time acknowledge the *power-to* you *do* have, take a pause, and perhaps a deep breath, and tell yourself a new story. Since it's up to you, make it a good one.

Be willing to learn

I am a woman and I have a child who identifies as a boy. Raising a child of the opposite gender has proved to be a learning edge for me. It has been a joyful, worrisome, and enlightening endeavor. In my home we have worked hard to excavate old beliefs and rewrite our inherited parenting manuals. We wanted to create an emotionally safe environment—a place where shame is close to nil, emotions are validated, and effective, kind boundaries are calmly held. It is not perfect. It's not easy. But it is possible. At the risk of delving too far into "how-to" territory, here are some suggestions that could apply to most small people, but are mentioned here specifically about boys/male identifying children:

Try:

- **Letting your boys emote.** Make safe, supportive space for them to feel their feelings. The healthiest thing for humans to do when they have a feeling is to simply have it.

- **Being aware of social conditioning (it's everywhere).** Larry Cohen, author of *Playful Parenting*, says it clearly, "Girls need extra opportunities to feel powerful and in charge, and boys need extra opportunities to feel connected and vulnerable."

- **Providing toys that bridge the gender gap.** Two of my closest friends had babies the same year I did. One male and the other female. For their first birthdays, I intentionally sent the boy a doll and the girl a toy car.

Avoid:

- **Telling them to "shake it off" when they get hurt— either emotionally or physically.** Repressing emotional release is stressful to the point of being a health risk. An emotionally unsafe environment is perceived as a threat just as much as a physically un-safe one, setting off that flight-fight-freeze survival state in the brain.

- **Calling your baby, toddler, or child a "little man."** This seems harmless, but it really lays the groundwork for messages and biases that encourage repression, competition, and violence such as, "Boys don't cry," "Be a man," or "Man-up."
- **Perpetuating sexist beliefs about boys.** Eliminate the statement, "Boys will be boys," as an excuse for bad behavior.

After working with children and families for over half my life, I know for sure that *emotions drive behavior*. Emotional states diminish access to the thinking, executive brain—the prefrontal cortex—the part responsible for weighing the consequences of your actions and planning ahead. When emotions are not allowed to run their course, brains are wired *away from* emotional intelligence. When we don't allow boys to feel a full range of human emotions—fear, anger, grief, delight, empathy—their emotional literacy weakens.

A culture of masculinity that shames boys for connection, vulnerability, fear, or sadness increases their social isolation, potentially escalating depression rates and violent behaviors. Every online source I checked put the rate of how many total violent crimes are committed by men at around 90%. I subscribe to the commonly held theory that this is due to their early conditioning, namely, being conditioned *to not feel*. It seems straightforward—if you are denied access to *how you feel*, your ability to be connected to, and have empathy for others, is diminished.

Wiring brains for the better

We are in a unique position as parents, teachers, caregivers, grandparents, and nannies to assist the next generation in having *very* differently wired brains. We can raise kids whose brains have an easier time communicating—who can bring calm and compassion more quickly. The next generation might have brains that are better at reading the emotional signals of others. Their brains can be empowered to have better boundaries and healthier relationships. As noted, I am not writing a manual here. There is no magic wand or formula, but it will help if you view your child as a whole and competent human—even in infancy. If you authentically connect with your children every day, you will see the positive impact on their behavior. Children can't survive on their own, and they know it. Because of this dependence, merely sensing disconnection from a parent can feel like a threatening emergency, which can fuel undesirable behavior. I'll talk more about emotions and limit setting later, but for now, know that it helps to reflect feelings to a child while intervening to stop unsafe behavior. You can say, "I can't let you hit your sister, even when you are really mad."

It helps to teach through example. Humans are social creatures, and children will eventually follow your lead most of the time. Ironically, even when you don't want them to. If we want to raise loving, helpful, respectful, human beings who can exhibit self-control and emotional regulation, well then, *that's exactly who* we *need to be.*

CHAPTER 2

The Most Important Relationship You Have Is with Yourself

"Beauty begins the moment you decide to be yourself." –Coco Chanel

If you're like me, you spent your 20s wandering the self-help aisle, going to weekly therapy, and sitting around a circle in uncomfortable seating at personal development workshops. No? OK, then I'll save you some time and money. Here's what I learned: I am messed up. We are all messed up. The whole world is pretty messed up. Love and honesty fix many of the messes. One reality of parenting is that our babies start so dependent and needy, and they do need us. *And*, we do *so much better* when we assess our needs before helping others. Chances are you learned the opposite: To give first and pay less attention to yourself. But that's not honest, and when you ignore your needs it leads to resentment, which is the kiss of death in *any* relationship.

How can we learn to put on our oxygen masks before we help others? I'm sometimes gasping for breath, struggling to assist the members of my family—wheeze, cough, sputter— did we lose cabin pressure? I am often in need of my own advice.

Bring on the kindness

As kind as I try to be toward myself, I know I can be kinder. I want to practice radical kindness. Blow-you-away kindness. Knock-your-socks-right-off kindness. Killer kindness and "kill-them-with-kindness" kindness. Because if I can rise to that, it means I have been taking excellent care of myself. I've been treating myself like a friend, attending to my needs, and acting in my own best interest. I have stopped beating myself up—with thoughts, words, or lack of attention.

When I take care of myself, I'm better at self-regulating and managing my energy and reactions. I am most able to do this when I factor myself into life's equation. This means trying to make sure everyone in the family gets *most* of their needs met *most* of the time. Babies and young children are particularly needy, and we obviously must take care of them, but try to get *everyone* on the roster. When you leave yourself off, you're more likely to get depleted. Instead, divvy up your attention and pay *some* to each person's needs. It's never going to be perfect, but a fairer division keeps you from becoming a martyr or throwing in the towel and yelling out of frustration.

Caring for yourself means knowing yourself better

When you pay attention to your emotional reactions and how you feel in your body, you can be more intentional with your behavior, because self-regulation is *hard*. Being kind helps this and every other situation. Kindness isn't "Pollyanna," or being in denial and only seeing the good. I'm talking about *being present*, paying attention, being real, and staying connected. That means you stay aware of your triggers—the things that really tick you off and get you emotionally heated.

Five apps to bring you calm, centering, and personal growth:
• Calm
• Insight Timer
• Breathe2Relax
• Headspace
• Sattva

You can probably guess the positive impact that kindness, awareness, self-regulation, and self-care have on the people you love: your children, partner, friends, and family. They help you set better boundaries and limits, which are so important. I always pair kindness with boundaries when I teach parenting classes. They go together like peanut butter and jelly. Many of us don't have a good working model of authority; often, we are elevated, agitated, or just plain angry.

My parents were usually furious by the time we pushed them to a boundary, bless their hearts. It's much more effective to know where the limit is, state it, and hold it *before* you lose your cool. Then you can be a more effective listener and coach for your children when the inevitable upset of confronting a limit follows. You can't blame kids for being upset about not getting what they want—that's human nature. But they will learn to accept a "no" gracefully as they mature, it just takes practice.

When I ask parents about taking good care of themselves, the answer I hear most frequently, especially from moms, is, "Yeah, I definitely don't get enough me time." Well, no. No one does. I think there's a better lens through which to view self-care. If you think of caring for yourself in terms of the time you get to do what you want—coffee with a friend, a massage, or ten minutes alone with a book (even though all those things are wonderful!)—there's more to learn. Because you *really* need to take care of yourself on a moment by moment basis and consider your needs throughout each day. In some ways, me time needs to be *all the time.* Sometimes we need to be a little, yes, I'll say it, *selfish.*

I can imagine some of you cringing at the S-word. Writer and activist Glennon Doyle says we need to be "full of ourselves" in the best way possible. We're strongly conditioned to not be selfish, or full of ourselves. However, understanding and prioritizing your needs *helps* your children and loved ones in several ways:

You know where you stand and can hold needed boundaries. If you are checking in with yourself, attuned to your thoughts, feelings, and rhythms, you'll know whether to say "yes," or "no," to someone's request. You'll be better at making decisions in general.

You retain a desired level of energy. If you make sure you're well fed, rested, exercised, etc., then you won't get so worn down. When you say "yes" to yourself, resentment is usually diminished.

You are more able to be the parent you want to be. It never ceases to amaze me how much more of a loving, kind, compassionate, connected, and fun parent I am when I have *filled my cup first*. If my tank gets too low, I'm cranky. If my child tries to siphon a gallon from me and I'm empty, I can't take it.

The way we treat our kids obviously matters, but the way we *treat ourselves* also leaves an impression. Don't children deserve caregivers who care about themselves and show it through regular action? Can we stay calm and steady in the face of discord and upset? Do we have a good sense of self and know our likes, wants, needs, and limits? What would it look like to model self-nurturance, self-regulation, and positive self-talk?

Give yourself permission to live life

Parenting is *busy*. Many parents work full-time, some more than one job. Others volunteer or have a side biz. Some of us are sandwiched between young children and aging parents who also need our care, not to mention the insane schedules of the kids! Some of you spend hours on the road every week, shuttling them to sports and activities—it's a lot. It reminds me of a note I once saw taped to a friend's bulletin board. It was handwritten in bold, letters: *If it's not a huge YES—say NO!* Saying "no" when no is warranted is an essential part of keeping your relationship with yourself healthy.

In addition to making good choices based on solid boundaries, maybe also slow down a little. Sometimes, when I try to do three things at once, I move so fast I bang into unclosed drawers and drop things on the floor. This can't possibly help me get out of the door any faster. Try doing one thing at a time and taking more breaks. Also, get out alone or with a friend or your partner. If you can't afford a babysitter, say "yes" to any trusted person's offer to help or try a child care swap with friends. As my friend Leah says, take the "exit ramp" as often as possible.

A little back story on my journey thus far

I started dating my husband when I was 23 years old. We were married three years later, and our son Josh was born near our tenth wedding anniversary. Before we became parents, we had thirteen solid years of relationship. Thirteen years of Dual Income No Kids: endless kid-free evenings, spontaneous long-weekend trips up the coast, and countless lazy Sunday mornings. I know it's a bit sacrilegious to wax nostalgic for the B.C. (before child) days, but to be honest, parenthood was a serious adjustment.

I did think about how different things would be once we became parents. I discussed it with a friend when I first started trying to conceive. She'd had her first baby in the verdant and fertile soil of new love and commented how nice it would be for my husband and me to start our parenting journey with a solid foundation between us. Even then, my response was something along the lines of, "Yeah, but imagine how used to *just the two of us* we are."

While the grass is often greener, I can see the wisdom of having some years logged in a union before taking on the massive project of creating, nurturing, and supporting a brand-new human being. And can we pause for a moment to acknowledge how *seriously* needy young humans are? So needy! And for so long! Eighteen years later a child is finally a grown-up (sort of). While you may never stop *being* a child's parent, at some point—not at eighteen, but maybe mid-twenties?—you do stop *actively parenting* them.

I am thrilled to be a parent. I *love* my son—the highs and lows, the joys, the challenges. This is genuinely the most significant commitment I can imagine making. Aside, I suppose, from the commitment to marriage all those years ago. I'm glad I made both, and there is probably no sweet spot or perfect time to have a child, anyway.

But relaxing, leisurely brunches on sunny restaurant patios? Yeah, I miss that.

Can you prepare for parenting?

Magda Gerber, founder of R.I.E (Resources for Infant Educarers), once said, "Parenting is a most difficult job for which you cannot really prepare yourself." Perhaps my first wrong turn was believing *I had* prepared myself. I'd spent six years in toddler and preschool classrooms and another six as a nanny caring for three young boys from tiny baby to four years old. My diaper-changing stats were off the charts, my soothing skills were top-notch, and I had naptime prowess. I had once majored in early childhood education, and I'd read *The Continuum Concept* and every parenting volume I could get my hands on.

Four must-reads for new parents:
- *What Babies Want* by Debby Takikawa and Carrie Contey
- *Your Baby Is Speaking to You* by Kevin Nugent
- *Welcome to the Club* by Raquel D'Apice
- *Let the Baby Drive* by Lu Hanessian

Everything I learned fueled my passion for understanding developing humans and drove me to promote respect and kindness toward children. In short: I had *plans*. My husband likes to remind me of the popular saying: *If you want to make God laugh, tell him your plans.* It was not pretty when reality hit.

As an example, here's merely *one* thing that didn't go according to plan in *one* area: breastfeeding. I had *planned* to breastfeed on demand. I tried, but he didn't seem to be getting enough milk or gaining weight. The lactation consultant's first home visit was three days postpartum. She diagnosed a tongue-tie that needed fixing. After a semi-traumatic visit to the ear, nose, and throat specialist, I had to use a nipple shield for months. For the uninitiated, that's a latex "straw" for an infant to use while they nurse. As Magda said, nothing—not even the best laid plans—can prepare you for parenthood.

Keeping the bar high, but reasonable

I have to admit that most of my first book, written mainly for parents, was completed before I became one. I finished final edits when Josh was a toddler, and while I questioned the feasibility of some of my advice (when did remaining calm get so darn hard?), I left the bar high, and will now spend the rest of my life trying to live up to my own standards. Luckily, I was also realistic in knowing that our kids will trigger us— though I couldn't have dreamed how often or intensely. My advice: If you mess up, apologize—it's the right thing to do, and it's great modeling. I have done it many, many times.

It's possible that the more I learn about parenting, the higher my ideals get, but I feel stronger in my convictions when brain research confirms that tiny, growing brains are wired as a result of adults' interactions with them. What we say and do *does matter*—a lot. It's not a perfect analogy, but it's almost like our children's brains are computers that arrive with hardware (nature) and then we slowly install the software (nurture). Connection and the ability to relate are at the crux of our experience as humans. And, how *we were wired as children* impacts how we respond—and react—to *our* children's emotions and behavior.

Dr. Dan Siegel, author of many parenting books, says, "The most important thing a parent can do is understand themselves." I'll say it again, *the most important relationship you have is with yourself.* Everything else flows from there, so employ strategies to nurture that relationship. You might need to patch things up with yourself. Some people find therapy, yoga, or meditation helpful. For others it's long walks, time spent in nature, or phone conversations with friends. Whatever it is, make the time. It's worth it.

Parenting is a marathon, not a sprint. I wrote that before I gave birth. Little did I know. *Labor* was a marathon. Parenting is an *Ironman*—a triathlon with grueling lows and endorphin highs—for the rest of your life. We laugh our heads off and cry our eyes out. We seethe with anger, fret with worry, exclaim in joy, drown in sorrow, and burst with pride. We shake our heads in wonder, and frustration. And we will keep going, no matter what. Because we are parents, and we are resilient.

CHAPTER 3

Fantasy Will Get In Your Way

"Children are not things to be molded, but are people to be unfolded." –Jess Lair

I hate to admit the fantasies I had about what parenting would be like. Visions of lighthearted fun with my child—always dressed in attractive and seasonally appropriate clothing—danced in my head. After over a dozen years taking care of other people's children, I knew there would be hard moments. But I didn't realize how different 24/7/365 parenting would be from punching out at 6:00 p.m. Let's say I had valuable skills, but no idea the stamina required. I know how to run, swim, and ride a bike, but that doesn't mean I can do a triathlon.

There are no parenting hacks

I saw a meme the other day that said something like "PARENTING HACK: Just kidding, there are no hacks. Everything sucks and these kids don't listen. This is your life now. ENJOY!" I laughed because it's kind of true. Children are wonderful, but they are also *a lot* of work. I do better when I keep my sense of humor. I mean, maybe there are some "hacks" out there. I did see the clever use of a laundry basket to corral a baby in the bathtub once.

Sadly, there are no shortcuts for the real work of parenting—the connection, emotional labor, and being there for your kids—getting to know who they really are. This work sucks the air out of the fantasy where everything is perfect, easy, and you make up for every disappointing thing that ever happened in your own childhood. Sorry.

These fantasies come from all directions. We think we won't yell and that our child will eat the meals we prepare. We imagine that our kids will get along, that they will be easygoing and cooperative. Things that aren't even on our radar turn out to be *so hard*. Breastfeeding, weaning, sleeping, toileting—simple things that seem like they shouldn't be that difficult—*so are*.

Five books of parent hacks and humor:
- *Go the Fuck to Sleep* by Adam Mansbach
- *Parenting: Illustrated with Crappy Pictures* by Amber Dusick
- *Parenting Hacks: 134 Genius Shortcuts for Life with Kids* by Asha Dornfest
- *Weird Parenting Wins* by Hillary Frank
- *I Just Want to Pee Alone* by Jen Mann, Kim Bongiorno, et al.

I thought setting limits would be easier

Like many parents, I struggle with setting limits, particularly around screens. Once upon a time, as an experiment, I enacted a "no screens during the week" rule. Josh was about seven at the time. And it worked, but only for a little while.

It went well until a long weekend when I slid the limit. Then I had a work deadline that led to the rule being further overlooked. The final downfall was letting him play with my phone on the way to school to get us out the door in the morning.

My boundary was pretty much toast.

Things were not going well. The ramifications of my lapsed limit became unbearable. I owned the problem and told him we would be going back to our original limited screen week.

The next morning, he asked, with a perfect combination of seven-year-old confidence and trepidation,

"So, can I have your phone on the way to school?"

"No," I said.

He whined.

I told him I understood his upset.

He argued.

I explained my reasoning.

He said he was going to find my phone and play anyway.

I acknowledged that he wanted to take charge of my phone and then shut my mouth.

He demanded the phone.

I said "no" again.

He stood by the kitchen table next to his half-eaten cereal, scowled, and said,

"If you don't give me your phone, I'm going to pick up this bowl and throw it at you!"

"I hear your strong feelings about wanting my phone. Please do not throw that bowl."

We stared each other down.

I took a deep breath.

Is what's going on here progress?

In my fantasies about parenthood, no one threatened to throw stuff at me. But I kept my wits about me because I have a good understanding of the triune (three-part) brain. If you haven't yet watched Dr. Becky Bailey's TED Talk mentioned in Chapter 1, please do. In a nutshell, triune brain theory says this: As our brains evolved and developed, our "human" brain—the cortex, thinking part—grew in addition to the "mammal" and "reptile" parts, sometimes referred to as the lower, or "downstairs" parts of the brain. The mammal part is the seat of the social-emotional brain and the reptile or lizard brain is concerned mainly with survival. It runs the fight-flight-freeze response that helps keep us safe.

Knowing this information about the brain tipped me off that my son was coming from an irrational place—his mammal brain. If I had fallen prey to *my* lower brain, I would have ended up yelling, or worse. As tempting as that is when kids act out, it will only escalate the situation. In this case, that might have meant a bowl flying at my head.

After getting myself calm, I could see his threat for what it was—just a threat—and a sign that he was stuck in his emotional brain. He was not rational, but he hadn't spiraled into a full-blown meltdown (flight-fight-freeze), either—a feat that perhaps should be commended. Children need very different parenting responses from us depending on their brain state (human, mammal, or reptile), nuance we can't pull off unless we're holding that viewpoint and managing *our* brain state too.

Later, when Josh got in the car for the ride to school, he asked a couple more times why he couldn't have my phone. I explained again and acknowledged how hard it must be to understand my reasoning. At that age, he couldn't possibly understand my adult perspective.

That's when I found myself complimenting him.

"I noticed you were able to control yourself and *not* throw that bowl this morning, even when you were really mad. You could do that because you're learning to stay in charge of yourself even when you feel upset." And because I like to offer a vote of confidence that he'll be able to get to the next level of keeping himself regulated, I added,

"Next time, you might even be able to just *say* how mad you are, instead of making threats."

I could have regarded his behavior that morning as un-acceptable. I could have made sure he knew *how* unaccept-able by dishing out shame, blame, or punishment. Instead, I chose to see his sassiness and threatening as progress, a huge step up from previous behavior like aggression or losing it entirely.

That morning was a reminder that raising a human being is a long game, and that I can always shift my viewpoint. I had the classic *How full is the glass?* question to answer for myself, and I chose to focus on *how far he'd come*, rather than *how far he still had to go*. The former felt better for me, and I'm guessing it felt better for him too.

The biggest fantasy: That I could keep pain at bay

It was such a blind spot to think things would go smoothly and I'd be able to keep my cool when things got hard. I didn't realize how tired I'd be. Or how angry I'd get. I had no idea how much it would freaking hurt. I didn't know that the stakes would feel so high, and the losses would be so significant and scary. Parenting can be terrifying and painful! *That* was not part of my fantasy.

It's almost like once you're a parent your pores open and more of life's stuff gets inside you. You can't screen out the horror stories of what happens to children because there is a small child on your lap now, and you can't help thinking, *Oh my God, what if that happened to him?* And that's only the unfounded worry! Other painful things are bound to happen.

Several years ago, we buried a family pet in the backyard. We were open about it. We petted the dead cat and put him in a box and talked about *The Tenth Good Thing About Barney* (Judith Viorst's wonderful book). It happened to be around the anniversary of my grandmother's death, but I hadn't made that connection until I was woken that night by the sound of

Five kid's books about death and loss:
- *Tenth Good Thing About Barney* by Judith Viorst
- *The Next Place* by Warren Hanson
- *The Invisible String* by Patrice Karst
- *Tear Soup* by Chuck Schwiebert and Pat DeKlyen
- *The Memory Box* by Joanna Rowland

my almost five-year-old crying next to me. He stood next to my bed shaking and sobbing. He could hardly speak and I was instantly alarmed. I felt his head for a fever, but he was not hot.

"What is it, Bubba?" I asked.

"When, y-y-you die and g-g-g-o to the u-u-u-universe, I w-w-won't be able to s-s-see you anymore." I could barely make out the words through his choking sobs.

I wanted to say, "NO! No, that *will not happen.* I will always be with you, and you will always be safe, and you don't have to feel this pain because life is rainbows and silliness and birthday cake and fun!" But that would have been a lie. That would have been hiding the truth; that life is both brutal and beautiful, or as author and activist Glennon Doyle says, "brutiful."

"Oh, sweetie, I know." I shook off my sleepiness and looked him right in his sweet face.

"Mom," he blubbered, "Wh-wh-wh-hen, you are d-d-d-dead, I will put up s-s-s-so many pictures of you."

I burst into tears. I burst into tears every time I read that and remember how sad Josh was that night. My boy. He woke up wondering how he'll cope when I die. He felt this deep sorrow and he came to me for support. So, I gave it.

"Oh, I know, I am so, so sorry." I hugged him tightly, and we cried. "Pictures are a really good idea. I know this is so hard to think about."

He cried and cried and I said nothing to talk him out of it. After a bit, I suggested that we go sit in the rocking chair in his room. He asked for tissues and curled up on my lap. We sat together in the glow of his red rocket ship night-light. We rocked.

My husband got out of bed and went downstairs. That got Josh thinking.

"I want Daddy to die first because I love you more, Mommy."

I didn't try to talk him out of that one either.

"I know, that's OK." And because I knew there was so much more pain underneath that statement, I reminded him softly, "You will miss Daddy too, when he dies."

"I know," he wailed, "When Daddy dies, who will make the stir-fry?!"

I held him while he cried.

He was grieving the eventual loss of us.

Losing your parents is a scary thing to think about. It's a scary part of life. I imagine that he feels less scared now because he felt some hard feelings and now knows he's not alone.

He felt things and survived.

Some day (hopefully, a long time from now), I will die, and my sweet son will lose me. He will have to feel the waves of pain wash over him. I only hope we have shown him that this is right and OK. I hope we've succeeded in helping him build emotional resilience. If he has practiced a thousand times with smaller hurts and losses, maybe he will be prepared.

> "Mum who is going to cut my nails when you and Dad die?"
> – Bobby, 5 years old

It will still hurt, but he will be ready.

Where is all this heading?

At some point our children grow into adults and leave home. It's hard to imagine that time when they are a baby, or a ten-year-old, or even a teenager. I asked several of my empty-nester friends to share their experiences, and my friend Nancy sent me this particularly poignant response:

"When my son left home for the first time, I was unprepared for the depth of pain I felt. It was almost physical, the "cutting of the apron strings" translated to a severing of an un-see-able, yet completely knowable cord between us. I knelt in my garden silently sobbing the day after we dropped him off at college; tears relentlessly flooding my eyes, face, and neck. This was grief, pure and simple. But it was an interesting grief. Not the typical type formed of the bleak and grey abyss of loss, but a grief that was made up of letting go, saying goodbye to the trappings of childhood, and welcoming the unknown. It was a scary grief, a reluctant grief, and ultimately a grief that ushered in acceptance and perhaps even a little hope.

I welcomed the peace and quiet of a house which no longer held the constant specter of teenage angst and its fallout aggression in the pursuit of longed for independence. I welcomed freedom from my own anxieties around whether I was "doing it right"—this parenting an adolescent on the cusp of adulthood. I welcomed giving it up to God, or the Universe, or whatever name one uses. I relinquished my duty to be ever watchful over my son's behaviors and choices. I welcomed the reduction in grocery shopping, laundry, and dirty dishes. I both welcomed and was saddened by the sight of his room, which remained in a pristine state: bed made, surfaces clear and organized.

Difficulty usually arrived in the quiet darkness of night. The intrusive images of my son, possibly facing some brutal reality, thrust upon him by life, fate, or at the hands of some malevolent person. This could easily have been chalked up to the neuroses of an overactive imagination. However, there comes a time when we understand our own life has been, and will continue to be, speckled with tragedies and hardships, and will be no different for our children. What gave me some semblance of peace was the hindsight that my own challenges did not destroy me, but in fact, make me stronger and wiser—a likely outcome for my son as well."

My fantasies about how I'll feel once my nest is empty included grief for sure, but I think more of a cursory grief, a "yeah-yeah, of course" grief. Now I'm thinking about the tears-flowing, snot-running kind of grief. And also, a big, *letting go* grief. This perspective from someone who's been there helps me remember to practice returning to the present throughout my days. I now understand more fully that it's all we really have.

CHAPTER 4

When Our Brains Work Against Us, Gratitude Helps

"Fall down seven times, stand up eight." –Japanese Proverb

When my 91-year-old grandmother had a stroke, I shared what was happening in an email to a circle of women with whom I'd been trading gratitude lists for months. It said: *My grandmother had a stroke and I am grateful I got here in time. It's 1:00 a.m. and I am at Maine Medical Center. Her name is Miki Matthews, and I would be even more grateful if you included her safe passage from earth in your meditations and prayers when you get this. Please hold my family and me in your hearts.*

I was astounded by how different it felt to experience loss, a death even, through the lens of gratitude. Much like a healing balm, gratitude took the sting out of the pain. Gratitude is not only about the "happy" parts of life, and it surely isn't about the perfect parts. It isn't even about looking for the silver lining or counting your blessings. It's about accepting *what is.*

The more I practice gratitude, the more quickly it comes. I recently learned the concept of "letting something rent space in your head," and while there are plenty of things I try to evict from my head, gratitude is not one of them. Gratitude is welcome to stay. Allowing space for gratitude shifts our perception of things. And since perception impacts reality, feeling grateful can transform your life.

Change your glasses when you sense negativity bias

As I understand it, we have a negativity bias to keep us safe. If we are always thinking the worst will happen and take a defensive posture, we'll stay alive. At least that's the theory—that this negative view is deeply encoded in our brains to help protect us. The worry, fear, and hypervigilance may keep us guarded and safe, but also caged, and frankly, miserable. If we know about this bias, that our brains trap us in this way, we can use awareness to shift away from the negativity.

Gratitude can be this new view, lens, or pair of glasses. They are glasses that, if worn regularly, will alter your view of the world. As author Dr. Wayne Dyer said, "When you change the way you look at things, the things you look at change." Again, is the glass half empty or half full? It seems like a simple question, but the answer isn't always easy. The answer is "both," and you get to choose. But we're often distracted by the activity and drama of our lives and we miss the choice. Gratitude brings a focus we can cultivate. It requires that we slow down a little and observe, you know, *actually pay attention*.

Everything I've read about gratitude puts it in the context of a practice. A few years ago, my good friend Kelly started sending a group of friends a daily gratitude list. I received them, loved them, and sent a few in return. But I didn't *commit* to it, so I didn't reap the rewards of practicing gratitude because I didn't, well, *practice*.

About five years later I was invited to join a group of women in a daily gratitude email exchange. My relationship with gratitude blossomed because of this

Three books for cultivating gratitude and kindness:
- *Attitudes of Gratitude* by M.J. Ryan
- *Random Acts of Kindness* by The Editors of Conari Press
- *The Little Book of Gratitude* by Robert Emmons

practice. First, there were *my* lists. They started short and sweet. I'd notice small things like the wind dancing through the trees, my contentment with my family, and my work situation, things like that. I might have fizzled out if it weren't for all the gratitude lists I had been *receiving*.

If I didn't get a dozen lists from a dozen different people offering a dozen different takes on gratitude, I would have bailed on my practice. If I were just jotting things down in a journal, I would have gotten lazy and stopped. But because of the group experience, I kept going.

If I got busy and missed a few days, the emails I received from others were impossible to ignore. My lists deepened and got more specific. I found myself taking stock of my day, not only as I sat to write about it, but in smaller, more aware bursts throughout the day. After a few weeks, I did see and feel the differences in my outlook. Even very tough days, I saw in a different light.

It was a couple of months into this practice when my grandmother passed away. Here is the full gratitude list I sent from my cell phone in a darkened hospital room the morning she died:

I am grateful...

That Rich was able to reach me before I left Portland and I could get to the hospital quickly. My 91-year-old grandmother had a stroke tonight.

For the kindness and comfort of modern medicine.

That my family is in agreement about her care even though she did not have advanced directives.

That I got here in time and could tell her I love her.

For the feeling of her warm hand in mine.

For laughter and tears.

For sitting vigil with my mom and sister, the beautiful "women's work" of death.

It's 1:00 a.m. and I am at Maine Medical Center. My grand-mother's name is Miki Matthews, and I would be even more grateful if you included her safe passage from earth in your med-itation and prayers when you get this. Please hold my family and me in your hearts.

Instead of trying to shield myself from the sadness, grief, and heartache of what was happening, I sunk right down into it. I felt it all. And when I did, I found all those things to be grateful for, even in my pain.

When you catch yourself gatekeeping

When I was five days postpartum my husband dropped me off for an appointment. As he pulled into the parking lot, I started to gatekeep—to feel like I knew best and needed to be in control. I asked what he was going to do if the baby got hungry during their short time at the grocery store (my hormonal worry and negativity bias shining through).

He replied, with a straight face,

"Not to worry, I'll just pick up some peanut butter."

Ha! Point taken. I laughed and was able to relax and *say goodbye.*

I first learned of gatekeeping from a mother for whom I worked as a nanny. She used the term to describe some-thing she was doing, while simultaneously stating that she needed to stop doing it. She said something like, "I know that my son and his dad need to have their own relation-ship and that my gatekeeping isn't helping." She was calling herself out, admitting to her overstepping of bounds. I had to go home and look it up, to make sure I understood its meaning: *gate·keep·ing 'gāt kēpiNG/: noun 1. the activity of con-trolling, and usually limiting, general access to something.* OK, I got it.

My second awareness of gatekeeping was a friend's stun-ning display of *not engaging in it.* She and I were chatting in her kitchen. I could see over her shoulder where her husband stood—he was supervising their eight-year-old daughter's attempts to put on a life vest. It was the kind with clips that come around in front and are difficult to click together.

I didn't see what portion of her flesh got caught in the plastic buckle, but I heard her scream and saw her start to cry. I cringed. But my friend—a mother of five, mind you—continued our conversation *as if nothing happened.* Only once my friend's daughter was attended to by her dad, and she came directly to her, did she offer any comfort. *She never even turned around.*

That was some rock-solid, non-gatekeeping mothering right there.

The scene sticks in my mind. How firmly she stood *in her trust* of both her child *and* her husband. It sticks with me how confident she was they could handle the situation and would consult her *if needed.* I remember her nonchalant response, and how it was nothing like what I imagined my hysterical reaction would have been had it been my child. (I was not yet a mother at the time.)

The whole situation was a heads-up I had some work to do.

The dominant culture's story places mothers at the helm of the caregiving ship and gives fathers menial jobs. I use the gender binary and these labels for ease in explaining gender bias, and to underscore caregiving assumptions because entertainment media is full of gatekeeping moms and bumbling dads—pick a sitcom, any sitcom. It's extremely easy for us to fall into specific roles. It's the water we're swimming in; we don't even notice it.

Not all parents have partners and gatekeeping relationships can also happen with grandparents and other caregivers. That said, most two-parent families have a primary caregiver and a secondary caregiver. I don't assume that in all cases moms are the former and dads are the latter. I am also aware that same-sex and gender-nonconforming unions and marriages will not have a mom and dad. In any case, it's a pitfall to watch for—the one where you think you know best and step in to correct and control the situation.

It may help if you start with gratitude. If you feel like you want to jump in and take over, take a breath instead. Then think of three things you are grateful for about your partner or the other caregiver. Gatekeeping is the result of fear—a crisis of faith—but also a lack of gratitude. Curb the desire to criticize and stay open to their way of doing things.

It has now become family lore—the time my husband took our toddler on a day-long outing. Upon their return, I asked if they'd had lunch, and he replied, "We had heavy snacks." I checked my irritation and the inclination to fuss because, guess what? Our kid was fine with heavy snacks.

Sometimes it's hard to be confident in yourself or your partner. Try to take turns leading. Practice stepping up and stepping back. Preschool teachers are known to say it's essential that children learn how to both lead *and* follow. Grown-ups need both of these opportunities too. If one person is always running the show, the other doesn't get a chance to practice and gain skills and competence.

When we step up or forward, we put our experience into action. When we step back, we give others the opportunity to do the same. If you are the primary parent, assume that your partner is way more capable than you think. Whatever it is, they can probably figure it out. Secondary parents and other caregivers, maybe don't ask for advice unless you really want it? Because whatever it is, you can probably figure it out.

Try leaning into discomfort

Have you seen the diagram of *Your comfort zone*, and *Where the magic happens*? If you haven't, go Google it. Or just know that the two spheres in the illustrated Venn diagram do not overlap *at all*. There's a reason for that:

- Comfort zone = Feeling safe.
- Feeling safe = Low risk-taking.
- Low risk-taking = Less magic.

That negativity bias pushes us to stay safe at all costs. Plus, many of us were taught to be risk averse as we were growing up. We got very clear messages: "Be careful," "Get down from there," and "Quit jumping."

These commands, aimed at our physical safety, are easy to identify. Others, the ones that most often drive perfectionism and anxiety, are more subtle: "She looks terrible in that outfit," "How could his parents let him do that?" or "Who told her she could sing?" Criticism, *even when aimed at others in front of us*, can severely impact how far outside our comfort zone we're willing to go. Sometimes we worry more about "fitting in" than feeling like we belong. We get in the habit of abandoning ourselves for others' comfort. I tell parents to try stepping out of their comfort zones for many reasons, but chief among them is that we are always modeling. If we don't show our kids, *with our actions*, how to take risks and stay true to ourselves, how will they possibly learn?

Five books on joy and happiness:
- *How We Choose to Be Happy* by Rick Foster and Greg Hicks
- *The Happiness Project* by Gretchen Rubin
- *How Much Joy Can You Stand?* by Suzanne Falter
- *10% Happier* by Dan Harris
- *The Book of Joy* by Dalai Lama, Desmond Tutu, and Douglas Abrams

We want *them* to take small and large risks. To raise their hand in class, speak up against injustice, and say "no" when a friend encourages them to do something stupid. But that means they will need to practice risk-taking in developmentally appropriate ways from a young age. It also means they will have needed to see *us* take risks. We'll want to stand up to Uncle Wyatt about his racist language at the holiday dinner, submit our writing or conference presentation, and sign up for that dance class we've always wanted to take. That will be leading by example.

Setting out to raise a new human is a potentially perilous endeavor. You'll consider the risks of a thousand weighty choices. There are decisions to be made around your child's healthcare, education, and religion (or not). There will be the agony of holding space for their pain after their heart's been broken and waiting up at night when they are out as teenagers.

Buckle up and be brave. Not by pushing past your fears, but through aligning *with your own heart*. That might mean practicing meditation or prioritizing rest. Or maybe setting a timer so you can pause throughout the day and tune into your emotional state. Because only when you drop from the chatter of your head, into the stillness of your heart, can you know what your next right move should be. Take the risks. Find the magic. Because as professor and poet Leo Buscaglia famously said, "The greatest hazard in life is to risk nothing."

Finding more joy

In one of her many amazing books, *Daring Greatly*, social worker and storyteller Brené Brown writes about her ten years researching vulnerability and shame. She didn't set out to study vulnerability and shame. She wanted to research *connection*, but when she interviewed people, what they shared were stories of pain, shame, heartbreak, and vulnerability.

Her research has shown that people who are *most willing* to lean into vulnerability and other mucky feelings feel *the most* connection and contentment in their lives. It's not the feeling, but *the protecting*, that makes us miserable. And it's the willingness and ability to engage with the hard parts of life—pain and shame, the very feelings many of us spend ample time avoiding—that *makes people happier*. And it wasn't actually happier that people became, so much as more joyful.

Another twist is that one of the ways we try to temper vulnerability and pain is to *turn away* from joy when we feel it. Silly, I know, but over 80% of Brené's research subjects reported feeling terror and vulnerability after a peak moment of joy. She dubbed this shield we attempt to use as "foreboding joy." This practice ran the gamut from "imagining the worst-case scenario" to "perpetual disappointment." She shared a story of standing over her peacefully sleeping children at night and feeling like she couldn't breathe for fear that something terrible would happen to them. Any mama can relate, but these fears consistently *drag us away from joy*.

The antidote to this foreboding joy? You guessed it! Gratitude. A muscle we can all exercise, one that will get stronger with each repetition.

Thank you.

Thank you.

Thank you.

CHAPTER 5

Listening Is a Superpower

"Our feelings are our most genuine paths to knowledge."
–Audre Lorde

I discovered Hand in Hand Parenting at the suggestion of a friend because my two-year-old was *wearing me out*. What I learned about listening blew me away. I knew from Pam Leo's book, *Connection Parenting*, her theory of the two metaphorical "cups" we carry within us. There's one cup that collects love and joy and another that collects hurts and fears. We were continually filling my son's "love cup" but could not seem to empty his "hurts cup" completely. He was touchy and demanding, and his tantrums were explosive. We held limits and offered empathy, but after twenty minutes, I would find myself out of patience and relying again and again on distraction, which worked, but only until the next insult. Once I applied Hand in Hand's five Listening Tools, everything shifted.

The Listening Tools lit a lightbulb in my head. I'd written an entire book about communicating with children that focused on *what we say*, while Hand in Hand Parenting's work brings to light the other half of communication: *listening*. The Listening Tools are used together to create and foster connection between you and your children. Connection with your kids helps them feel safe and relaxed, like you've "got them," a skill that will impact to how they *hold themselves* when they're

More resources from Hand in Hand Parenting:

- Website: Tons of articles and courses at www.handinhandparenting.org
- Book: *Listen: Five Simple Tools to Meet Your Everyday Parenting Challenges* by Patty Wipfler and Tosha Schore
- Booklets: *Listening to Children* by Patty Wipfler

older. Your relationship with your child also affects how much influence you have on their choices and behavior. We have zero control, but *through our relationships* we can support and guide. These are the tools:

Special Time is one-on-one time where you let your child choose and guide the play or activity. Some people call this "time-in," as in the opposite of a time-out. There are a few wise guidelines for making this time successful. First, set a timer. Remember that your goal is to follow your child's lead. I had no idea how much back seat driving I was doing in my kid's playroom until I attempted Special Time. It's harder than it sounds, so knowing that it's going to end in 15-20 minutes helps you stay present and attentive. Special Time provides a deep sense of safety. And children who feel safe are more likely to be cooperative. This daily time with each of your children works like a charm, I swear.

Staylistening is a tool for when your child has "flipped their lid" and is in that lower part of their brain. Maybe it's the mammal brain, but probably it's the lizard brain—they've lost their ability to think clearly. A parent's job in this scenario is to stay as close as possible (keeping yourself and them safe) and ignore their ridiculous behavior. Then, beam them with love and attention with your voice, words, body language, and facial expression. Listen without reacting to their messy, strong feelings. Convey total confidence they can survive the intensity, that they are safe. Because the only way out is through.

Is this hard? Yes, it is. My first go left me exhausted. My child's ability to cry and rage for *so long* surprised me. I had curtailed his emotional expression for *my* comfort and when I didn't, he doubled down and really went for it. My husband and I sat on opposite sides of a carpeted room—holding space together, listening. His tantrum lasted for over an hour. *An hour.* Once I let go and trusted that this was OK, I could relax a little. I believed the process would be cathartic—that allowing the feelings (and stresses and tension) to come *out* would make him feel better. And it did. Every time we Staylistened after that got shorter and easier. We trusted ourselves to stay calm and regulated, and Josh believed he could get through his mucky emotions.

Setting Limits is a vital part of parenting because children's brains are still developing. They are terrible at assessing risk. It's our job to keep them safe from the dangers of the world and the dangers of angering us. We need to know where our limits and boundaries are (as noted in Chapter 2) because if we set limits *before we are upset*, it's easier to hold them without harshness. When paired with Staylistening, limits give your child the chance to offload the emotions that drive their off-track behavior. It's wonderful to set boundaries with kids, but as I said earlier, unfair to expect them to like it. Be ready for the upset because it's perfectly normal. Limits can even be set in a lighthearted way that brings laughter, which leads me to...

Playlistening is where you get some laughter going with your child (but no tickling). They say laughter is the best medicine for good reason. It helps reduce stress and improves our health. It's an excellent way to off-load lighter tensions and worries too. While crying hard often brings a sense of emotional lightness and relief, laughing hard can do the same. Start early and apply this tool liberally. Be

> "Mommy, is my butt still there? Daddy said I was gonna freeze it off!"
> –E.E., 3 years old

silly. Take the less powerful role. Get goofy. Make up ridiculous characters. Use outrageous accents. Play dumb. Be a sloth. The possibilities are endless. Whatever makes your child laugh—*do more of it.*

Listening Partnership gives you a way to nurture *yourself* for the seemingly endless and often exhausting work of parenting. The bottom line is that it's tough to provide the level of listening and compassion outlined above if *you too, are not receiving it.* Listening, exchanged with another adult—preferably not your parenting partner—who will, a) not judge, and b) not offer solutions or advice, is a real fuse extender. Parenting is stressful and our number one job is to manage that stress so we can model self-regulation and offer our kids our best selves. No other practice or self-care strategy I've tried has been as effective as regular Listening Partnership. It doesn't matter what you talk about—whatever's "up" usually does the trick.

It's also helpful to crack open your inherited parenting manual. What, this old thing? Yes, dig in! On page 23 you may find how sass was handled when you were young. Page 68 could reveal that when you were four and had a tantrum, you were ignored or told, "Stop crying or I'll give you something to cry about." These kinds of memories are good to explore in your Listening Partnerships as they could be affecting your parenting.

These five Listening Tools used together provide a virtual map for navigating the intense emotions that arise while raising a family. You'll reduce stress and enjoy your kids more, creating a more peaceful home and family life.

What happens when you take coercion off the menu?

One fine morning when my child was about three-and-a-half (everything they say about this age is true, by the way—the brain's busiest time), he *flat out refused* to get dressed. I had to get to work, and he needed to go to preschool, but he was in full resistance mode.

He fussed and ran away from me.

He flopped his body on the floor and rolled around.

"NO!" he repeated, again and again.

Loudly.

He was out of control, and to be perfectly honest, I didn't know what to do. I was frustrated and annoyed because none of my cajoling or firm boundary-setting had worked. I'd finally raised my voice and he was hiding under a nightstand in the corner of my bedroom. I felt *my* self-control slipping away. At my wit's end, only three remaining strategies came to mind:

Force. I could physically overpower him and shove him into his clothes. But at 30 pounds that could end badly, especially if I was mad while doing it. Unless it is truly to keep them safe, never touch a child when you are angry.

Threats. I could threaten with some punishment, removal of a privilege, or other unpleasantness.

Bribery. I could offer to reward him with a treat or desired activity.

But, and it's a big but, none of those responses would strengthen my relationship with my child. Not one of them would bolster our connection. In fact, they would all break and potentially damage our connection. And here's the thing, each of the three approaches above breaks connection *because it is coercive in some way*. I knew if I tried any of those approaches, my child wouldn't gain new mastery over his emotions, moods, or behavior. He wouldn't learn anything other than *the adults are in charge, and I should obey*. He wouldn't get to think or choose. He certainly would not feel empowered to get dressed.

But, on that day, I couldn't think of anything else. And I knew I didn't want to do what I *was* thinking.

So, I did nothing.

For the moment, I admitted defeat.

I looked over at my son.

He looked back at me.

I sat down on the floor.

"I don't know what to do," I said.

He looked at me.

I looked back.

I sat there for a minute (it felt like more than a minute). And in that moment of *pause*, I remembered that connecting was the goal. I asked myself, *How can I drop everything else, skip the power struggle, stop fighting for control,* and connect?

It came to me suddenly. I looked down and saw my son's blue and white muslin "lovey" blanket. He'd dropped it while skittering, *still in his PJs,* to hide in the corner.

Of course, Playlistening! I thought to myself. *Laughter and fun, I'll start there.*

I picked up the blanket and, with a twinkle in my eye, threw it toward my son. He caught it and looked over at me. He threw it back.

I tossed it back to him, this time right at his face.

He giggled and threw it at *my* face. We both laughed.

"Oh no you don't!" I said, laughing and tossing the blanket toward him again. "I'm gonna get you!" I yelled as I jokingly lunged at him, giving him a big hug.

And guess what?

Once we were laughing and relaxed, I was able to steer him toward his room and into some clothes so we could *finally* get out the door. He moved from *resist* mode into *let's get moving* mode. My three-year-old's behavior was entirely in control! No force, threats, or bribes necessary.

Staylistening during tantrums

Tantrums are strong emotions that come out in a large explosion. All these feelings are acceptable. All feelings are valid—sadness and grief, frustration, anger, and rage. Small hurts, fears, and worries can build up. I often dwell on, *what's this tantrum all about?* However, I find that this only distracts me from being fully present with my upset child. When I check my judgments of rude, unreasonable, and out-of-proportion, I can do a better job guiding him through his difficult feelings.

Sometimes, the hurt or fear from a challenging circumstance we think our child has handled well will come out in a seemingly unrelated tantrum. One morning when Josh was about five, he woke up on the wrong side of the bed. Out of the clear blue, he asked me about a specific kind of fruit snack that I had once bought him.

Once.

And months ago.

As I stretched and woke up, he continued to ask me about the snack. It took me a minute to catch on that he was cooking up quite an upset. I had not bought him this fruit snack, and boy, did he want it.

"I know which fruit snacks you mean. The twisty ones?"

"Yeah, those twisty red ones—I want one right NOW! You have to get them for me," he demanded in a wound-up, cranky tone.

"No," I said, keeping my voice gentle and low, and *not mentioning his rudeness at all*, "We're not going to have those."

"YES, I WANT THOSE FRUIT SNACKS!! I WANT THEM RIGHT NOW!!!!"

"No," I repeated, my voice firm and gentle, "we won't have them."

He lost it. He thrashed his body around the bed, trying to kick me and growling with rage. I held a pillow between us and told him I needed to keep my body safe from his kicks. He cried and wailed and kept kicking. I kept myself clear of his impact and didn't argue with him. I observed his body and breathing and kept us both safe.

I did not shame him for losing control. I didn't get mad that he was making an unreasonable request at 6:30 in the morning or freaking out about being told *no*. My mantra was: *He has big feelings and they will be done when they are done.* I imagined how powerless he must have felt in the dentist's chair earlier that week. After the appointment he'd said it, "hurt more than a little," yet had not shed any tears. I poured my attention where he must have needed it. After a few more minutes of him crying, trembling, and sweating I said,

"Do you want to come in my lap for a hug?"

"Yeah," he said, crawling over.

He got in my lap and cried hard for a few more minutes. Then he tensed up and demanded the fruit snack again. After I told him *no*, he went back to struggling.

"Hey, I have an idea," I said, a few minutes later, "you're having a lot of angry feelings. Why don't we go into the other room and use a blanket to help you get through them?"

He agreed and we walked down the hall together.

"I'll roll you up in this blanket, and you can fight your way out. It will be like a giant swaddle." He agreed and I rolled him up in the blanket—snugly and safely. He grunted and fought, and finally popped his arms up and wiggled his way out.

"You did it!" I yelled.

He did it three times and then he wanted me to try it. I pretended it was *really* hard to get out and asked him to help me. When I finally got out, I acted *so* tired, like I could barely move.

"Do you want to do it one more time?" I asked. He did. After that, I suggested we go downstairs to have breakfast and get ready for school. He followed my lead without a shred of resistance.

It might seem like a lot of work (and highly indulgent) to permit kicking and yelling and loud, messy feelings. But, here's the payoff—my child then felt calm, centered, and ready for his day. It took all of twenty minutes, and the fruit snack topic disappeared *completely.*

It wasn't important that I figured his upset was probably about the dental visit. Getting a cavity filled is definitely no fun and that may have been the cause. But what was most important was my ability to stay present and calm while he moved through his emotions. Try to go with whatever gets you present more quickly. If you can think of a reason, great. If you *can't* think of a reason, then let that go and reorient to where you are—helping your child with some overwhelming feelings. When I did that for my son, he could move forward knowing that these feelings, *and the expression of them,* were accepted by the adults in his life. Then he felt accepted and safe in the world again.

Mission accomplished, until the next opportunity for skill-building arises.

CHAPTER 6

Emotional Competence Is Not a "Soft" Skill

"Do the best you can until you know better. Then when you know better, do better." –Maya Angelou

One day, my seven-year-old got frustrated with his LEGO® creation. It had broken, as these creations tend to do. He saw this as a personal attack and lost his temper. I offered to help. He declined and tried to fix it himself. It broke, and he lost it. I empathized and again offered my assistance. He said an extremely clear, "no" and started yelling about how stupid the toys were. I let him. I let him rant and rave. I let him try and fail to get the "stupid, dumb thing to STAY TOGETHER!"

"Why do they make them like this?" he wailed.

I said nothing. God knows I've asked myself the same question many times.

I gave him some space and stood back a little. I wanted to see what he was going to do next. He grabbed the pillows off the couch—one by one—and threw them on the floor in a fit of rage. *Pillows! Excellent choice, kid.* I let him own the problem and work his way through his feelings. And he did, all by himself. I sat on a nearby chair and offered validation. That was it.

I kept my mouth shut, which was a hard-won victory.

What are these strong feelings, and why are they important?

Emotions can be a flood that sweeps us off our feet. Or at least out of our thinking brains. In this example, my son's feelings were an overflow of frustration, born of his inability to get the small and delicate pieces to do what he wanted. From a neurological perspective, emotions are messages. They are our brains and bodies in communication with each other.

Remember, when we feel scared our brains send chemicals into our bodies that say, "Prepare to fight!"—or run, or play dead. It's that downstairs part of the brain. When we feel frustrated or hurt, our bodies wisely get upset, tantrum, shake, or sob so that stress hormones dissipate and we can return to emotional equilibrium. When emotions are acknowledged, expressed, and moved through, we can get back to our thinking brains. This process is an important component of self-regulation. Our brains naturally mature as we age, which is why most of us don't continue having (frequent) temper tantrums our whole lives.

The importance of self-regulation

There are many things parents benefit from practicing, but perhaps none as important as self-regulation. Self-regulation is what happens when you find yourself headed into that downstairs brain, and instead, maintain your ability to think. It means you're able to weather a difficult situation that is rife with emotion and still maintain your equilibrium. It's feeling an emotion fully, without letting it sweep you off your feet, so to speak. It takes dedication and practice.

Five children's books about emotional regulation:
- *Some Days I Flip My Lid* by Kellie Bailey
- *Mean Soup* by Betsy Everitt
- *A Little Spot of Anger* by Diane Alber
- *I Am Peace* by Susan Verde
- *Puppy Mind* by Andrew Jordan Nance

Also, if you *do* lose it (your thinking brain, control of yourself, your equilibrium), self-regulation is *getting it back more quickly*, and recovering without beating yourself up or heading down a road paved with guilt and shame. When adults can do this in front of children, it's awesome modeling.

Self-regulation is a complex process. I perceive myself as generally calm and patient, and maybe I am. But, when something sets me off, I feel *justified* in my anger. It always feels right when *I* am upset, because they're *my* feelings. I fall into blame and think, *That person shouldn't be so irritating*. It's not typical for me to ask myself, *Why am I so irritable?*

I define self-regulation as the ability to stay in charge of yourself when you have intense feelings. According to Stuart Shanker, author of the book, *Self-Reg: How to Help Your Child (and You) Break the Stress Cycle and Successfully Engage with Life*, it's all about understanding stress and managing your tension and energy levels. Self-regulation is *not* the equivalent of will-based self-control.

Let me say that again: *I am not talking about self-control.* That would involve *increasing* your effort and will, which in turn *drains* your energy and *reduces* your ability to self-regulate. That's why I like to tell parents and teachers, "You can't fake calm!" Self-regulation is the thing that helps us not freak out or see a child's whining as a reflection of us. It keeps us calm in the face of a toddler's tantrum, an aggressive kindergartner, or a rebellious teenager.

Self-regulation allows you to listen to your child's upset feelings, support their motivation, and guide their behavior. It affects your ability to respond, set boundaries, and foster healthy relationships with your children. This ability is also crucial for kids, and ironically, they need the adults around them to demonstrate it for them to learn.

Once we understand Dr. Shanker's five domains of self-reg, we can build skills ourselves and pass them along to our kids through both modeling and teaching. The five domains are: biological, emotional, cognitive, social, and prosocial. I recommend reading his excellent book, but keeping an eye on these separate areas, and how you may get depleted in each of them, will help. I might be well-balanced in meeting my biological and social needs but be depleted in the other three areas. This practice of keeping tabs helps us stay even keel and might look like paying more attention to our stress and worries, minding our own hunger and fatigue levels, practicing deep breathing, and *not* taking things personally during meltdowns (theirs and ours).

I also have a three-step strategy that can help you increase your ability to self-regulate:

1. **Notice your emotions.** Nervous. Mad. Frustrated. Annoyed. Every feeling creates a sensation in your body. Whatever it is, notice it as soon as that first blush moves through your system. Irritation might feel like warmth on your face or quickened breath, or it could sound like an escalated tone of voice—that's your clue you've moved into an emotional state.

2. **Watch for the story.** Here's how it plays out for me: My son resists going to bed because he wants a snack. I get irritated and a story flies into my head. It's not usually a verbal story—or a cohesive one with a beginning, middle, and end—so pay close attention. Mine sounds like, *This is total B.S.! I should not have to put up with this. I already offered him a snack. Why is my kid always hungry? Why won't he go to sleep and give me peace? Why!? Why!!??* If bedtime is breezy for you, insert your problem area—getting out the door in the morning, child care drop-off, negotiating outfits, meals, dental visits, whatever. Everyone has something that escalates their child and pushes their buttons.

3. **Change the story.** Start with, *This isn't personal*, because it isn't. If I catch myself (that's why watching for the

story comes first), I can reframe the whole situation and self correct my perpetual *Why me?* narrative into something more empowering, kind, and sane. I might think, *I wish this kid was a better sleeper. But, alas, this is my child, and I can't change the fact that he fights sleep. Let's take a deep breath here. Maybe he just needs to cry, had a rough day at school, or is extra hungry because he's having a growth spurt.*

Anything is better than the victimized, powerless story I told myself the first time. Everyone's internal dialogue is different, and maybe your shift could be like one of these:

- Instead of, *How dare she reject the food I worked hard to pre-pare!* Try, *Kids have picky palates for an evolutionary reason.*

- Instead of, *Why won't he put these clothes on, for Pete's sake?* Try, *He is so confident in his desires. He knows what he loves to wear.*

- Instead of, *This child is the clingiest one in the bunch—why so much whining?* Try, *Let me see if I can fill his emotional cup with love and attention.*

That's it. Notice the emotions. Watch for the story. Change the story. It shifts how you show up to interactions with your family. With practice, children feel their feelings fully and then recover their emotional balance too. They intuitively understand when emotions disrupt the sense of well-being and safety they typically feel. One of the wonderful tools they wisely (though unconsciously) use to help them recover their thinking and regulated state is tantrums. It turns out that tan-trums help kids learn to regulate their emotions—another important reframe.

Building our emotional competence

The tricky and cool thing about being a parent in the 21st century is that we get to learn how to regulate our emotions *while* we're teaching our kids to regulate theirs. I'm learning new lessons about my patterns and abilities all the time. A few years back, I found myself blissfully lying on a massage table. I was in a calm self-care reverie, and despite my best efforts to let go and relax, my train of thought sounded like this:

Ah, summer will be winding down soon, but that's OK. Maybe I can get another one of those cute kid-sized Adirondack chairs on sale like the one my parents got for Josh. Did I ever take that chair out of the car? Huh, I don't think so. Did I unload the car last night and bring in the things from the farmer's market? I don't think I did. Oh crap, everything I bought has been in my car for the past 18 hours.

Any mom can relate to this.

We forget stuff.

All. The. Time.

But what happened next was progress for me. I was able to observe my thoughts and emotions from a "witness" perspective. My internal dialogue continued:

I can't believe I forgot all that food in the car! Wait, what is that sensation? Is that a rush of shame flooding through my body? Why yes, it is. Wow, that's ridiculous. It's just wasted food; it wasn't a child I forgot, or something else important. Is that fear closing my throat? Huh? Why am I feeling so scared and ashamed right now? Sure, I flushed thirty bucks down the drain, but it's only money. It's not the end of the world.

Because I was in the middle of reading Dr. Gabor Maté's book *When the Body Says No: Exploring the Stress-Disease Connection,* I had recently learned the term "emotional competence." Much like emotional intelligence (EQ), emotional competence refers to the ability to feel and identify our emotions. It means we're able to express those emotions and learn what they are trying to teach us about our needs and boundaries, and then take action on both of those fronts. It's a skill that invites us to notice whether an emotional reaction is due to something happening in the present, or if its origin is in the past, stemming from an unmet childhood need. Emotional competence is essential for human beings to thrive.

Emotional competence, or lack thereof, is taught and conditioned in us through our early experiences. How the adults in charge of *our very survival* felt about our expression of feelings impacted whether we accepted these (all) parts of ourselves or abandoned and disowned them. If mom or dad sent the message that it was *not OK* to cry or fuss, then guess what? We absolutely learned not to. If we were punished for things that were out of our underdeveloped mind's ability—forgetting things, making "stupid" mistakes, etc., then our brains created fear-response wiring as a result of those experiences—*and it never went away.* My internal berating of myself is totally unhelpful, and yet I find myself doing it. I feel trapped in a cage that is no longer locked.

The painful *aha* was in asking whether the feelings I was experiencing were from the present, or the past. I noticed how I felt, and I also noticed that it was an *old* reaction to being forgetful and making mistakes. This was newly forged emotional competence.

I am a grown woman who spent thirty dollars of *my own hard-earned money* at the farmer's market. When I realized I'd accidentally left my wares in the car, where they got ruined in the summer heat, my body flooded with a cortisol, stress, adrenaline response. Maybe it was because I was lying down and feeling relaxed that I saw this response so clearly as old, as outdated; *as absurd.*

I felt like I was going to get in trouble, like I had done something *hugely* wrong, that I was a complete failure for not remembering the groceries. I also felt a strong pull to hide the event. To throw away the food and pretend it never happened. I wanted to avoid facing the shame I felt. Instead, I felt the feelings as thoughts streamed through my head:

*Why was it such expensive food I had to forget about. What a waste—all that food—thrown away! My husband will be angry! Did I really just think that? No, he won't. He's made plenty of expensive mistakes, this is no big deal. And even if he is...*oh well. *This is old childhood conditioning. I was not permitted to make child-sized mistakes. The expectations were off and the emotional price too high. I must have forgotten because I'd already brought everything into my parents' house on my way home. After we had dinner there, I took it from their refrigerator and put it back in the car. Given that I'd already unloaded it once, it makes sense that I forgot when I got home.*

That last part, where I was desperately trying to figure out *why* I messed up, the reasoning and rationalizing—it's torture. It didn't matter *one bit* why I forgot. I just forgot, something that every human does from time to time.

Several tears streamed down my face. I felt such compassion for myself, for my parents, for *their* parents. Generations of people have been raised with shame, pain, and fear as huge parts of their experience. *There is no reason for this.* It is detrimental to our relationships with ourselves, with our kids, and according to Dr. Maté, it's damaging, not only to our mental health, but our immune systems as well.

There is no behavior for which a child deserves to be humiliated, punished, or shamed. *Ever.* There are much better ways to guide children, to understand their behavior, to set boundaries, to listen to feelings, to model what's right with empathy and love.

Then I grieved. Which is the appropriate response to a loss.

It was a small loss, a $30 loss.

A $30 lesson.

Frankly, I would have paid much more for it.

CHAPTER 7

Kids Behave That Way for a Reason

"You cannot make people learn. You can only provide the right conditions for learning to happen." –Vince Gowmon

I brag that in one area, early child development, I had it going on. I knew developmental norms inside and out by the time I had my baby. And it helped. *A lot*. I knew that the persistence of a new toddler was totally normal. I expected the negativity of a two-year-old. I was ready for my preschooler to come apart at *his very seams* over the smallest problem. I knew, so I didn't take any of it personally, and that was a gift. But, as soon as my child was a little older, things got sticky. Without the developmental knowledge, it was way harder to relax or parent effectively.

Is this normal?

I now scour the internet for articles on tween development and the impact of hormones and puberty. I can relate to parents everywhere who look at their child, cock an eyebrow and wonder, *Is this normal?* It helps to remind myself daily that his brain is not fully developed yet and that kids will be kids. But now that I'm far beyond my comfort zone, I get it. I understand that sometimes the behavior just seems... ridiculous.

Is it normal that they disappear into their headphones for hours at a time? Even if it's just to listen to music or an audiobook? I hope so. Is it normal that they snap, "What?" when you call their name. Apparently. I'm sure we're all tempted to think our child is the only one—the kid whose behavior is atypical and will turn out to be a terrible person or a criminal. But it's unlikely that's true. Especially if you've been treating them with dignity and respect since they arrived. If you're worried, get support. But a lot of what we see as troubling kid behavior, is actually typical kid behavior.

Kids are supposed to act like kids

I have a message for all parents, especially the moms and dads of screaming babies, melting-down toddlers, demanding preschoolers, sassy school-aged kids, and grumpy tweens and teens. I guess I'm talking to everybody when I say, "Your child is not bothering me." Your child is a child who is growing and developing and is surely doing the best they can in any given situation. I get that. Most people get that. Yes, there will be the occasional upturned nose. Yes, you may catch a glare or an exasperated look from the *one* person in the crowd who has never been a parent, teacher, or aunt. But most people understand because *they have been there*.

What if we didn't panic about disturbing the peace? What if you could see that many more people are sending you compassionate, understanding glances, or mouthing, "I've so been there," or offering some other show of solidarity? It takes a village, remember?

Take a deep breath.

People who don't want to hear a child cry at the grocery store, ever, should move to one of those adult-only condo villages where they can live happily ever after and never hear the delighted laughter of a child. Because you can't have it both ways. You and your children have a right to exist, on good days and bad ones. To make noise even; to be seen and heard.

Also, your child is not in my way.

People apologize for a child being in the way. Or correct them sharply to watch where they are going. I *like* seeing children out in my community. That's part of what makes a community a community. I stopped and had a friendly conversation with a little boy at the grocery store on a pre-pandemic day. His parents had tried to hustle him along, so he wasn't in my space, but he ended up helping me count out the limes I was purchasing. We all smiled and went our merry ways—it was lovely.

Try to curb the message that's often sent to children that they don't get to take up space. Even your huffing and puffing teenager is OK with me. I used to *be* a huffing and puffing teenager. And a whiny preschooler. And a screaming baby. Immaturity is the hallmark of young people. Neuroscience tells us that the highest functioning part of the human brain (prefrontal cortex) is not fully wired and developed until the mid- to late-20s. Human childhood is crazy long.

Crazy. Long.

But that's OK! Our long childhoods are exactly what allows us to be big-brained and mature (for the most part) as adults. And who doesn't sometimes struggle with adulting?

A new parenting paradigm is upon us—one of healthy attachment, developmental understanding, allowing for growth to unfold, and holding space for emotions. This new lens helps us to not moralize, demonize, or pathologize our kids' behavior. It helps us *not* take their upset and aggression personally. It helps us feel closer to them.

As mentioned, our parents *did not* have the benefit of understanding this. They most likely came from a background where children were seen and not heard. Most people thought that punishing children for their immaturity was the best way to help them *be* mature, or that bribing them with rewards for "better behavior" was an avenue for bringing maturity. Nope.

Luckily, we now have new, helpful information about why kids act the way they do. Behavior is communication, and sometimes the message is, *I'm little and immature, and I'm also doing the best I can. Love, help, and guide me, please.* Or, as the parenting program *Circle of Security* advises parents, "Always be: Bigger, Stronger, Wiser, and Kind."

We are the grown-ups and we have the power to change things.

We might need to edit our parenting manuals.

Sometimes our struggle to be mature is a direct result of maturity being pushed on us too early when we were young, or safety not being offered, or shaming punishment we received for being immature or "behaving badly" as kids. This approach is based on the misunderstanding that children need to be bribed with a reward or prodded with a punishment. We can stop this cycle and heal these hurts.

It's not common for parents to fret about children's physical development. Each child has their curve on the chart. The same holds for their emotional development—they will get there. Send the clear message that they are doing just fine. They get to be young and immature, for now.

One day they'll have grown and matured. As if by magic. They will be tall (maybe taller than you), and they will startle you with their vision and compassion. Their steady gaze and wide-open heart will show you that you have succeeded.

Adjusting your expectations

Many, many parents have unrealistic expectations. ZERO TO THREE, the nonprofit organization focused on early childhood, conducted a survey of over 2000 parents in 2016 and found that a majority of them believe children can control their impulses in early childhood. Unfortunately, this is much earlier than brain science tells us is possible. We *want* them to be able to share, have impulse-control, and manage strong feelings. These are all goals most humans meet in due time (though not soon enough for weary parents). It will help if we are more patient, take a deep breath, and remind ourselves, *If they could, they probably would.*

You might rely on your memories from childhood when considering development, but your recall is probably not that accurate. You might be *sure* you learned how to be a good loser when you were four and your sister won eight games of *Trouble* in a row, but that was probably the time you ended up under the kitchen table crying. You didn't *actually* learn that lesson until you were closer to nine. You think you were five when you learned to swim, but maybe you were just walking on your hands in the kiddie pool (I know I was). You're certain you were able to put yourself in someone else's shoes and empathize in fourth grade, but in reality, you didn't get that lesson 100% until...wait, did you ever fully get that one?

Your kindergartner calls you a poopyhead. Your 13-year-old rolls his eyes and lays the sass on thick. Your three-year-old gets up from the dinner table endlessly. Your toddler won't stop sticking her fingers up her nose. These are perfect examples of kids being kids—certainly in ways that irritate adults, but they are such typical behaviors, teachers use the term *developmentally appropriate* to describe them. How you react, or better yet, *respond*, will influence not only how often you'll see these actions, but how children *feel about themselves* for exhibiting them. We create a self-fulfilling prophecy when we shame, bribe, punish, and lecture. We send the message that they are wrong for acting in these normal, though undesirable, ways.

What happens when parents can stay relaxed in these button-pushing situations? Remember Playlistening? It's possible to keep your cool and bring on the laughs. Say, "What? Poopyhead again?" Pause to reach up and touch your head and bring your fingers to your nose. "Ew, gross. I guess I'll have to go wash my hair." Roll your eyes back at the teenager and say, "hashtag sass factor 3000," in your best SoCal accent. For the preschooler who won't stay at the dinner table, try a happy, warmhearted, pretend "gluing" of their bum to the chair, with lots of hugs when they try to escape over and over again. Tell your nose picker, "Wait, let me grab a flashlight and see if I can find the boogers up there."

These responses bring laughter and create a more positive self-fulfilling prophecy, one that trusts your child's inherent goodness. You can assume that your child is doing their best with the tools and brainpower they've got. Perhaps aim to inspire internal motivation instead of blind obedience. How about an *I-know-you-can-do-it* type of prophecy? Or an *I-trust-you-to-remember-on-your-own* prophecy. Wait just a minute before you nag or prompt. Be patient, they will learn.

Try trusting your child, adjusting your expectations, and relaxing a little. I know how hard it is, and I'm guessing your kid is a good kid and will do the right thing. They are trying their hardest. Painful as it is to watch, mistakes are how humans learn.

What it can look like when you meet them where they are

Sometimes it's hard to explain the differences between old paradigm and new paradigm parenting. What does it mean to shift away from anger and annoyance as a parenting strategy? What does it look like to engage in a fresh way? How can we be the changemakers that will raise a generation that does not go straight to beating themselves up when

Five "new paradigm" parenting books:

- *Joyful Courage* by Casey O'Roarty
- *Peaceful Parent, Happy Kids* by Dr. Laura Markham
- *Positive Parenting* by Rebecca Eanes
- *The Danish Way of Parenting* by Jessica Joelle Alexander and Iben Dissing Sandahl
- *What Young Children Need You to Know* by Bridgett Miller

they make a mistake or take a misstep? How can we have more peaceful homes, more reliable connections, and more mentally healthy citizens?

I don't know the answers to all those questions, but I know growth is possible and reflecting on them can help you to effectively reparent yourself. Children always benefit when parents bring awareness and intention to their interactions with them. This reflection from a parent who attended a workshop with me says a lot:

> "Just have to thank you again for the workshop last night. I was able to effectively use some of your ideas this morning. An example: we are all jet-lagged, and the kids are having trouble getting out of bed and getting going. We have been helping them get up and dressed these last couple of days because of that. P really didn't want to this morning. She was sitting on the couch and I was holding out my hand to take hers and help her into the bathroom, and she started waving a foot at my hand in a kicking motion. I would typically start getting frustrated right there. But instead, I said, *'Oh, I wonder what that means. Does waving a foot mean you need 6 kisses on your left ear?'* And she BEAMED. She said no and waved the other foot and made up something that meant...but that's not what matters. It's the beaming that means everything. I'm getting teary now writing this. She was tired and grumpy and didn't feel like she had the energy to get moving, and I made a connection that really helped, instead of creating tension and making things harder. It makes me sad to realize that's often what I do. So, I really want to thank you for the reminder and for the tools."

This is the kind of change that's possible with awareness and intention. *It is possible, and it is sustainable.* You can make life-altering changes in your relationships with your children that will bring more peace, connection, joy, and love to your home. Now, and well into the future.

CHAPTER 8

The Double-Edged Sword of Modeling

"Children learn more from what you are than what you teach."
—W.E.B. Du Bois

When my son was about four years old, I noticed he made this obnoxious sound when he was irritated. Like when I'd ask him to do something he didn't want to do, this back-of-the-throat, cough-like sound would erupt from him. It was kind of an *I can't even* sound; it sounded a little like the word "yuck," but without the "y." It was a clear sign that he felt totally put out by whatever was happening. I know, at age four, right? It was super annoying. Then one day, I got frustrated and rolled my eyes and *the exact same sound* came out of my throat.

Yeah. So, I had to stop doing that.

Our children learn a lot from us

They ask us many questions, and we certainly do our best to answer. We also teach in other ways, like when we provide our kids with new materials and experiences. But we are teaching our kids 100% of the time in another huge way—through our actions. Some things are best taught through example, so why not take advantage of the fact that our children are *biologically inclined* to attune to us and imitate our every move?

There are many areas where you can put a little attention and end up teaching your child a whole lot. For one, respect. Sure, we can ask our kids to respect us and others. We can prompt them to use polite words and a kind tone of voice. But, how do they really learn respect? By receiving it, that's how.

I know it can be hard to remember that drooling toddlers and defiant preschoolers (not to mention feisty school-agers and surly teens) are intelligent human beings, but it's true, they are. Development and emotions push their behavior in directions we dislike, but if we remember their wholeness and humanity, we can respond with more love and respect.

Also, humility. Because we want our kids to know how and when to admit they are wrong. When they're young and totally full of themselves (and not in the good way), they tend not to do this. That's where your consistent modeling of admitting fault and apologizing comes in. Our children need to know we're human and make mistakes, just like they do. Since we have the more fully developed brains in the relationship, *the onus falls on us to go first*. Admit it when you mess up. Say you're sorry. Mean it. Make amends if needed and move on. They will eventually learn to do the same—what a valuable lesson.

I've already talked about emotions quite a lot. Children feel them intensely, just as we once did, before we perhaps learned that expressing strong feelings was frowned upon. It seems like it would be helpful to show children that we can "maintain" and keep it all under wraps, but that's not authentic. Kids need to know that emotions are OK—fear, sadness, grief, anger, joy, delight—these emotions are all part of being human. As social creatures we are wired to tune into the feelings of others. When we cover up how we feel, our children *still know how we feel*. This can be a fine line since we don't want to burden our children with our emotional reactions *to them*. But full denial of what you feel isn't helpful, it just confuses them and sends a mixed message. Instead, try sharing your feelings by honestly showing and talking about them in a developmentally appropriate manner.

It is a double-edged sword that your children are always watching you. What you say and do speaks volumes—aim to be a positive, but not perfect, example. Your kids will thank you.

Eventually.

You might have to model a little patience first.

The many faces of fixing

There is one thing that many of us do that sabotages our relationships. It can impact our relationships with our children and our parents—siblings, friends, coworkers—everybody. It's something that I happen to really, *really* love doing. It leaves me feeling competent and helpful. Some people even appreciate when I do it. (That's what I tell myself, anyway.) As a parent, its draw is *particularly* irresistible. The siren song of...fixing.

Sometimes I call fixing being helpful, offering a solution, or giving my point of view. Other times I call it advice, an opinion, or problem-solving. But really, I'm just trying to fix things because it will make *me* more comfortable. No one likes being around someone who is upset, or in pain, or angry—that's because we're wired to attune with each other. When someone else is out of sorts, we feel it! That's the blessing and the curse of being connected to one another. It's the price we pay for intimacy and empathy—*we have impact on each other.* I want to be tuned into other people's feelings, but I don't like it when they are cranky or upset.

What I really need is better boundaries

When my boundaries are squishy, I forget to do what I know will be most helpful. I don't stop talking, lean back, and just be. I forget that holding space is sacred and helpful, all on its own.

I meddle.

Even when I know that the number one, most empowering, truly useful thing I can do is give people (small or grown-up) my trust that they will get through their feelings.

Yes, sometimes that person (ahem, nine-year-old) is noisy whilst going through their emotions. I still don't have to *do anything.* What if I let it be? What if I kept quiet or only murmured things like, "That must be hard," or "I hear you."

What if?

One day we were at the farmer's market without a lot of time. We ran into friends and my son played on the playground while I picked out tomatoes, cucumbers, and fresh herbs. With my bags of veggies weighing down my arms, I told him it was time to go. He held up his one remaining honey stick and tipped his head to the side.

"But I wanted to get some more honey sticks."

"Oh, I'm sorry, we need to go now."

His shoulders dropped as if they had weights on them.

I got tense and stern and told him again we needed to leave.

He hemmed and I hawed.

I ushered him toward the car. He moped and I felt the heat of irritation rise in my chest.

Then I remembered: *I don't have to fix this problem.*

He felt disappointed. We didn't have time to go back to get more honey sticks (I was right about that—we pulled up to his noon recital at 11:59 a.m.).

All I had to do was have a good enough boundary to ride home with a cranky nine-year-old. Once I knew that was my job, I could do it. And, of course, once I was calm and relaxed about what was required of me, he settled down and moved on.

Sometimes I forget I'm not managing an inconvenience

I often implore my son to, "Please practice patience," when waiting is necessary. Then I snap at him, "I'm losing my patience!" when he makes me wait. I want him to move from playtime to mealtime to bedtime with ease and on my timetable while I tell him, "Just wait a minute," or "Hang on a second while I finish this email."

I tell him, "You're not listening to me!" and "You're not paying attention."

Oh, but *I* am the one who is not paying attention.

People often say, "He's just doing that to get attention."

Yeah well, that's because your attention is required.

Pay attention!

Pay attention when he says, "I want to tell you something."

Pay attention when they say, "Watch me Daddy!"

Pay attention to the way she looks up at you and says, "I want to hold your hand Mommy," as she steps out of the car. This means she has listened and integrated the lessons you've been teaching.

Pay attention when they fall apart after losing *Go Fish*. This means they are too young to be a good loser. Perhaps skip the lecture? Maybe you can get them laughing if you apologize profusely and make a jokey, heartfelt promise to lose all the rest of the games.

Pay attention when he asks for every toy in the store. Notice that he is likely overstimulated or needs a good cry. Offer the warm, firm limit that you are not buying any toys today. Acknowledge that this is hard—this wanting and not getting. Last I checked wanting and not getting was still hard. Even for those of us with mature, adult brains. For his small, still developing mind, it might be unbearable. This and many other all-too-human lessons will be learned in good time and will be best absorbed as you stay connected and loving.

As breastfeeding expert Kittie Frantz said, "Remember, you are not managing an inconvenience; you are raising a human being."

Remember in as many moments as you can.

Inconvenient behavior is your child saying, "Please, pay attention."

When you're modeling (which is always), even small course-corrections help. When I reflect on my behavior and reactions,

I find there's always room for growth. If I pull myself out of the hole of, *boy-I-really-blew-that*, and *what-a-slow-freaking-learner-I-am*, then I can more easily (and gracefully) move forward. Because self-recrimination is a trap, try not to hang out there. If you find you've fallen in, shut it down as soon as you notice it. A gentle, *Oh whoops, look at that—beating myself up again—I've learned that's not useful. Move along, move along,* should do.

Small shifts. Made often.

That will keep your ship steady and head you where you want to go.

When your modeling is not so great

My child recently challenged me to take a 24-hour break from social media. After much experimentation, we'd limited his access to screens, and he'd reached the ripe old age of *being able to point out blatant hypocrisy*. So yes, that's wonderful, and I said OK.

We decided from 7:30 p.m. to 7:30 p.m. and I don't recall why. My husband thought this was cheating since I was not removing myself from an entire news cycle, or something like that, but whatever. Lessons were learned and that's all that matters.

Three books about managing screen time:

- *The Art of Screen Time* by Anya Kamenetz
- *Raising Humans in a Digital World* by Diana Graber
- *Screenwise* by Devorah Heitner

Lesson #1: I don't even know I'm doing it. I was checking Facebook and Instagram on a totally unconscious basis. Within the first few *hours* of my screen time break, I found myself on my phone to do something (check email, send a text—both still authorized) and was suddenly *reading a status update.* Hello? What the heck? The first time, I shut the app quickly and rode the waves of shock and shame. The second time, I moved the icons to a separate section so I could not see them. Because apparently, I was not at all in charge of my own behavior—such bad modeling.

Lesson #2: It's severely limiting my creativity. The day I was off Facebook was a Sunday. Right away I noticed that I had some stretches of time where I was alone with my thoughts. I was like, *Oh yeah, this what it feels like to have space to think!* I'd been limiting my ability to ponder and reflect. To chew on an idea. You know all that stuff that *makes one a decent writer.*

Lesson #3: Comparison is the thief of joy (Theodore Roosevelt already knew this). Not long after my little experiment, I saw a meme in my Instagram feed about how after hours of scrolling, one ALWAYS feels so much better about their life. Ha! *Not.* I'm all for people showing the best parts of their lives on social media. I love cheering on my friends and watching others succeed. But I'd be lying if I said I never took an emotional hit from seeing someone's warm and sunny vacation photos on a sub-zero Maine day. Or a photo of BFFs when I'm feeling lonely. Not to mention the state of the world—those updates can be a little overwhelming and terrifying these days.

Lesson #4: It's severely limiting my productivity, time connecting with others, and sleep. If I am scrolling, scrolling, scrolling all non-working hours of the day and night, that is time I am not doing something else. Something else like reading a book. Or having a conversation with my spouse. Or playing a board game. Or calling a friend. Or getting to bed at a decent hour. Or writing a blog post. It's not good for me. It's not good for my marriage. It's not good for my friendships (even though it does "keep me connected" to far-away peeps).

It's also not good for my relationship with my child, or my parenting. The endless stream of information is totally distracting. So, I'm putting tighter restrictions on my social media time and aiming to bring myself back to the present moment (again, and again, and again). That, and the screen time limits function on my phone are the only things that seem to help.

Sometimes I model bad behavior on purpose

Confession time: We allow full on swearing in our home. From the tween. Yes, even that word. And that one. And that one too.

Truth be told, the first time my child said the F word he wasn't even two, and he was parroting me. Great modeling, I know. But in my defense, it was 2:00 a.m. and I was really fucking tired. I attempted to clean up my act, but honestly, I love to swear. I find it to be fabulous stress relief, and unless you are swearing *at* someone, or they've specifically requested that you not, I don't see the harm.

Once our boy entered preschool, we revisited the subject and decided to teach him another important concept: situational awareness. I've borrowed this term from whatever it really means (something to do with law enforcement and maybe Jason Bourne?) and applied it for my own purposes. Here's what I told my four-year-old when he got to repeating my curse words at home:

"Bub, those are strong words. They are powerful words because our culture says so. It's important for you to know that most grown-ups will be very upset if you ever say that in front of them."

"But not you Mommy?" he asked, looking me straight in the eye.

"No," I answered honestly, "not me."

So, in the same way my child learned that his teachers would not cave to whining but I sometimes would, he learned that he could swear at home, but not at school. It has never, not once, been a problem. If I can let my language, behavior, and actual hair down at home, why can't he? Which leads me to a problematic double standard. If you step back and think about it, kids have it tough. They're expected to hold it together and be on their best behavior all the time—at home, at school, in the grocery store, on the street, at Grandma's house, whilst attending a classmate's birthday party—pretty much *everywhere*.

This is just plain unfair.

Listen, I get it. We want our children to end up competent, socially aware, generally polite humans. But here are my two-pronged two cents:

1. Our kids need a break. They deserve some time and space when we loosen our standards, stop focusing on their behavior, give them room to breathe, and for the love of Pete, *let them be in a cranky mood for once without getting completely annoyed.* Imagine if your partner or friends *always* expected you to be chipper and cooperative. Just. Not. Realistic. We all have varying public/private personas and behaviors—it's OK for kids to, too.

2. If our expectations are too high and/or unreasonable, your children are definitely going to blow a gasket at some point. You don't want that to be at school, in the grocery store, on the street, at Grandma's house, or whilst attending a classmate's birthday party. Because of this, my philosophy is to make *all kinds of space* at home for child nonsense, *with* teaching and coaching so that the previously mentioned situational awareness can be achieved. I *want* my child to ask himself, "Is this sleepover a good place to make a fart joke?" and answer, "Maybe not."

Remember to take a deep breath when your little one says "poop," or "stupid," or worse. I'm pretty sure you're in good company, and if you permit space for a little raw, uncensored behavior at home, maybe your kids won't have quite so many tantrums at the grocery store or at your mother-in-law's house.

CHAPTER 9

Creating Inclusive Communities

"Not everything that is faced can be changed, but nothing can be changed until it is faced." –James Baldwin

We speak about the village in which we wish to raise children. We know that parents need support, preferably "the right number of adults" with whom their children can have relationships. But many families don't have the type of close-knit community the word *village* suggests. On a recent stay with friends my son yelled, "Mom" and three people answered. That's probably a good ratio, but most of us don't live with that every day. When I think of a village, I imagine an idyllic, safe, and folksy place where people know and trust their neighbors. I have visions of children running in slo-mo from house to house across bright green lawns. I'm not sure this type of village ever existed, and if it did, I'm sure it came with its own set of problems. Fantasy and fuzzy history aside, families need connected relationships—among each other and within their communities.

Our village has become the whole world.

If we learn nothing else from the global coronavirus pandemic and racial justice upheaval of 2020, let it be this: We are an interdependent species—we rely on each other for our collective well-being. I will quote Glennon Doyle again, she says, "There is no such thing as other people's children." We must learn to cooperate and care for one another.

Sometimes we succeed in showing up, and sometimes we fail. We will no doubt continue to be tested by other threats and viruses, and we will need to continue to rise to the occasion of fighting against racism, sexism, and for social justice. I wonder, *How can a different kind of parenting help?* Parenting that improves the parent-child relationship impacts children's beliefs, abilities, skill-building capacities, and worldviews in positive ways.

I believe we can transform the future by adjusting how we raise children. We have the power to influence how our children see the world and how they see other people. Ones who look like them and ones who don't. The people in their own neighborhoods and the ones on the other side of the planet. How can we parent against nationalism, bigotry, misogyny, transphobia, homophobia, and hate? Here are some suggestions:

Model good relationship and communication skills. I know I've talked about modeling a lot, but that's because it is: *So. Very. Important.* Keep in mind Jeree Pawl's quote, "How you are is as important as what you do." When you show up every day with an open and loving heart, you show your children *how to be.* Each time you own your emotions and communicate clearly, you show them *how to behave.* When you prioritize relationship health with your partner or co-parent (if you have one) you continue to set an important example for your children.

Model good boundaries. When we set firm limits with children, we demonstrate what boundaries look like. When we respect the boundaries of even tiny humans, we lay the foundation for learning about consent. When we are clear about where we end and they begin and accept emotional expression, we help them understand that their strong, messy feelings are OK with us. Good boundaries are what differentiates attachment from enmeshment. When children understand boundaries and go out into the world, they will also know to respect others' limits and set their own.

Resist using punishment as your go-to discipline method. I've already spoken to this, but it's worth mentioning again. There are many reasons why empathy, connection, and guidance work better than punitive ways of attempting to teach kids. Punishment makes kids miserable, and while we believe this will help them learn, feeling badly always brings *their* misery sharply into focus. This misery, left unsupported, could hamper self-regulation and increase anxiety and depression. Additionally, punishment fuels self-centeredness and reduces empathy.

More resources for pushing back against toxic masculinity:
- Documentary film: *The Mask We Live In*
- Book: *Boys & Sex* by Peggy Orenstein
- TED Talks:
  - *How I unlearned dangerous lessons about masculinity* by Elda Jackson
  - *The Mask of Masculinity: the traditional role of men is evolving* by Connor Beaton
  - *Why I'm done trying to be "man enough"* by Justin Baldoni

Parent against gender bias. In her important book, *The Mama's Boy Myth*, Kate Stone Lombardi highlights an increasing number of mothers who are raising strong and healthy sons by *keeping them close* and helping them gain important social and emotional skills. As discussed in Chapter 6, these are not soft skills. We all need these skills to get along with each other. Remember my story from Chapter 1, where I bought my friend's daughter a car and my other friend's son a doll for their respective 1st birthdays? In addition to offering children "opposite gender" toys and experiences, you can step fully into the role of helping others manage *their* discomfort when your son is carrying a baby doll in a sling.

Monitor how you talk to young children about their bodies and sexuality (especially girls). You would be shocked if you knew how often your ice breaker with a three-year-old girl is about how she looks or what she is wearing. I'm embarrassed to admit I'm guilty of it myself. In addition, another pet peeve is joking about needing a shotgun to protect teen girls or noting how much of a heartbreaker a boy might turn out to be. These are outdated paradigms that don't serve children in their development.

Teach your children about sex and sexuality. These are fundamental parts of who we are as humans and we can banish the shame from them. Shame breeds disconnection, and disconnection feeds hate and violence. Get the support you need and find someone to talk to about what makes sex and sexuality hard to discuss with your children—you could cultivate your Listening Partnership. There are legitimate reasons we don't feel very comfortable with these topics. Our culture sends dreadfully mixed messages, and avoids the reality that sex is pleasurable. Last I checked, it was pretty typical for people to grow up and want to have sex. You can help lay a healthy foundation by naming body parts with anatomical words as early as possible and cultivating a relaxed ap-

Three guides for helping you talk to your kids about sex:
- *Girls & Sex* by Peggy Orenstein
- *Sex and Sensibility* by Deborah M. Roffman
- *Birds + Bees + Your Kids* by Amy Lang

Five books about sex for kids of various ages:
- *It's Not the Stork* by Robie Harris
- *It's So Amazing* by Robie Harris
- *It's Perfectly Normal* by Robie Harris
- *Sex is a Funny Word* by Cory Silverberg
- *Where Willy Went* by Nicholas Allan

proach. Research found that knowing proper names for private parts (penis, scrotum, vulva, clitoris) potentially protects children from perpetrators. See sidebar for additional resources.

Normalize that gender and sexuality differences are reality. When you matter-of-factly tell a young child about gender differences and explain that people of all genders can love whomever they want, they will think it's no big deal. Explaining what being gay or transgender is to a child is *comfortable for them if it's comfortable for us.* Here's an example of a simple anti-bias move I've always made when we play the board game, *Life.* When we stop at the church to get married, I ask my son, "Do you want to marry a boy or a girl?" Then I give him the corresponding pink or blue peg for his car. He asks me the same and this is now completely normal to him. With regard to gender, it may seem strange if you and everyone (you think) you know "fits" into the gender binary, but this is not the case for everyone. If you feel decidedly male or female, and you were born with the corresponding genitals to *match* that feeling, you are cisgender. Some people are not. Our kids are growing up in a world where it will soon be standard to ask someone upon meeting them, "What pronouns do you use?"

> "My mommy isn't a lesbian! My mommy's gay!" – 8-year-old child

Teach that *diversity* is the norm. If you are part of the dominant culture (white, straight, cis) you may feel that you are "normal" and everyone else is "different." But that's an ethnocentric, heteronormative perspective—a bias. It's estimated that between 4 and 10% of Americans are LGBT, and did you know that according to NBC, non-Hispanic white people now represent roughly 63% of the U.S. population? According to a 2013 Bloomberg article, the majority of American babies born in the U.S. are non-white. Whites are already in the minority in my home state of California.

Avoid teaching kids to be "colorblind." When you do, you lose the opportunity for many rich conversations, plus, kids *aren't* blind. If they see differences and we ignore them, it creates an incongruence that's puzzling. Point out differences and talk about them. We are *not* all the same. And sadly, our world is not one where all are treated equally. We have a responsibility to work on becoming antiracist so we can help our children become antiracist too. Professor Beverly Daniel Tatum notes in her best-selling book, *Why Are All the Black Kids Sitting Together in the Cafeteria?*, that racism and white supremacy are a pervasive smog we all breathe growing up in the United States. If you don't expressly work *against* white supremacy, you will absorb it and pass it on to your children.

Five books to help grown-ups cultivate an antiracist lens:
- *So You Want to Talk About Race* by Ijeoma Oluo
- *How to Be an Antiracist* by Ibram X. Kendi
- *Me and White Supremacy* by Layla F. Saad
- *Raising White Kids* by Jennifer Harvey
- *When They Call You a Terrorist* by Patrisse Kahn-Cullors

Acknowledge discrimination and privilege. Point out injustice. Promote media literacy and notice how much more white people are represented in the mainstream media. Question the poor representation of racial and ethnic diversity. Notice and discuss the demonization of dark-skinned people in Disney® and other movies. Speak up about the unfairness that needs to end. You can leave reviews about children's content at *www.commonsensemedia.org* to help other families and to screen your own media consumption.

Read books that depict all kinds of people and families. The best resource for locating diverse books for children is the website *www.diversebookfinder.org*. But please refer to the

Four children's books that depict LGBTQ families, diversity, and awareness:

- *This Day In June* by Gail E. Pitman
- *And Tango Makes Three* by Justin Richardson and Peter Parnell
- *The Family Book* by Todd Parr
- *ABC A Family Alphabet Book* by Bobbie Combs

sidebars for additional book lists. Having these books in your homes and schools is especially important if you don't live in a diverse community. Humans are diverse. Reality is diverse. Our planet is diverse. Ask your local schools and libraries to have these books on their shelves. You help your children understand their world more easily and comfortably when you normalize differences from an early age.

Embrace diversity whenever possible. Avoid the assumption that white is the norm. Look for toys and picture books that include people of color. Unfortunately, this is harder than it should be and you can note that as well. Also, remember that history can always be told from many different views. When you tell children "facts" about our cultural past, try the caveat, "This is the commonly told story," or better yet, research and share multiple perspectives.

Five children's books that address racial diversity:

- *My Nose, Your Nose* by Melanie Walsh
- *Shades of People* by Sheila M. Kelly and Shelley Rotner
- *The Colors of Us* by Karen Katz
- *I Am Mixed (I Am Book)* by Garcelle Beauvais and Sebastian A. Jones
- *Mixed Me!* by Taye Diggs

This list of suggestions is not exhaustive. There is so much parents can do, especially white parents, to create inclusive communities. Chief among them is examining our own internalized racism, white supremacy, and bias. This is not just about parenting your own children, it's about normalizing the everyday tasks that are required to change the status quo.

Mermaid Blue and other ways of making impact

No matter where you happen to live, a metrosexual, gender non-conforming male is commonplace. Where I live in Maine, I see men with two earrings or wearing eyeliner on a regular basis. I also catch a glimpse of some nail polish from time to time and it makes me smile. Sadly, a boy wearing pink can still turn heads. Some boys/male identifying kids are still given a hard time for long hair, or misgendered as girls—mine included. Yet, it's socially acceptable when girls/female identifying kids play with trucks, wear blue jeans, or have short hair and play sports. Why is that? Here's my answer: homophobia and misogyny.

Three books that help tell American history from varied perspectives:
- *Americans Who Tell the Truth* by Robert Shetterly
- *A Young People's History of the United States* by Howard Zinn
- *An Indigenous People's History of the United States for Young People* by Jean Mendoza, Debbie Reese, et al.

In our culture, it is more accepted for women to express masculine traits than it is for men to present in *any way* as feminine. This difference might have something to do with the fact that in our society women, femaleness, and femininity are devalued, feared, and hated. And femininity of any kind in boys and men gets perceived as gayness.

Why are we so afraid of this?

I don't care if my son embraces his feminine side, or worry that he might be gay, with the one exception that some people are so intolerant of these things that they would want to purposefully harm him. Even when we aren't homophobic because we are afraid of homosexuality, we may still fear the discrimination, bias, and downright hate it could bring.

Why do we continue to perpetuate the stereotypes that require our little boys to suck it up and be a man? If a child is gay, asking them to hide it will not make them any less gay. Don't we want our children to be at ease with themselves? I am comfortable with my son's honest expression of self. I want him to be fluent in the full range of human emotions. Why are these traits seen as feminine?

When he was a toddler, my son discovered a pair of my grandmother's clip-on earrings. He was so excited to try them on. I watched him shake his head and delight in the sensation as they swung back and forth on his little ears. Even though they pinched a little, he refused to take them off until naptime. When he woke up, he asked to put them back on right away.

But before we headed into the grocery store, I told him that dress-up time was over. I soothed my cowardice with a story about how I wouldn't let a little girl wear such grown-up earrings in public either. The truth was I didn't want him to get any dirty looks, or have an overbearing person say something to him about how boys don't wear earrings. I guess I thought he was too little at the time to understand this—that it would be too hard to explain other people's beliefs.

A couple of years later, a friend innocently posted a photo of her three-year-old daughter's freshly polished toenails. They shone bright pink above the caption: *Mother-Daughter Pedicures*. This adorable photo (it was undeniably cute) got me thinking. My son loved to dress-up and to adorn temporary tattoos. He'd been known to cover himself from head-to-toe with washable markers. I knew he would love nail polish, so I bought a bottle of non-toxic blue polish at Whole Foods. (Was I chickening out by getting blue? Maybe.)

After his fingers and toes were shimmering in Mermaid Blue, I casually told him, "You know, *I* don't think so, but some people believe nail polish is only for girls and women." When he asked me why, I told him I didn't know. I might have said something about that viewpoint being outdated and misinformed and he nodded as if that made perfect sense.

We're all on a learning curve

It takes work to watch for your prejudices, and it helps every time you talk to your children about these topics and address bias, privilege, and power imbalances. When you acknowledge whiteness and white supremacy and discuss diversity in all its forms: gender, sexuality, differently-abled, and neurodiversity (the autism spectrum, attention differences), you make the world a safer place for more humans. This is good because it's possible you are raising a gay, neurodiverse child and you just don't know it yet.

When you adopt an antiracist stance, you improve safety for the children in your home and neighborhood. You reduce dichotomous thinking and hard-to-see implicit bias. Because, as I've already highlighted, *we are always modeling for our children*. We model with what we say and what we don't say. Children see who we shy away from and what seems to make us feel uncomfortable. They notice when we're relaxed and what gets us heated. They can likely discern who we love and, yes, those we fear. If we reduce anyone's humanity with our actions or words, our kids pick up on that. They know.

FINAL WORDS OF WISDOM

"We have more possibilities available in each moment than we realize." –Thich Nhat Hanh

None of us knows what we're doing or where we're going. Not really. No one has ever raised children in this time, right now. The world has recently gotten *very* unpredictable. We can't possibly know what kind of adult lives we are preparing our kids for, but we'll do our best to care for ourselves as we care for them. It may mean swimming against the cultural mainstream to treat everyone in our home with respect and kindness. Parenting matters because relationships matter, and our relationships with our children will last a long time.

If you play more, they'll cooperate more

"Mummy, it's good that man-eating tigers only eat men, isn't it?" –Leo, 7 years old

Play is the first language your child speaks. When we nurture play in children it helps them become fluent. When we tune in and play with them— really connect and really play—we offer them a well of *worthiness*. Babies and kids receive that loving attention and get the feeling that they are *seen* and that they *matter*. The good news is that this foundational connection is one parents can make and nurture over and over. The great news is that many, many parents do play with their children—a lot. We know that play is good for kids, but it's great for grown-ups too. And there are even ways that play can help us out as parents.

Preventive play can improve child behavior. If you set aside just ten minutes a day to engage with your child around something they are interested in, and follow their lead in play, you will fill their love and connection cup. This kind of play is a stressbuster and helps them better regulate their easily tipped emotional equilibrium. I mention Special Time again because it can be your number one meltdown prevention strategy—*it works*. Remember the four guidelines: No distractions (phones, etc.), follow the child's lead, play at their level, and don't have a plan or agenda.

Play and humor can help diffuse difficult situations. When your kids push your buttons (potty talk or a bold attitude), you *can* take the high road and respond with a playful approach. If your kid says they're shooting farts at you, duck and run for cover. Yell, "Oh no, the farts are after me—engaging fart protection mode!" I guarantee your child will laugh, which is likely all that's needed to break the tension. If they get defiant and refuse to get ready for bed, pretend you are a servant, and you'll be fired if they don't comply, "Oh dear, oh dear! My boss will be back soon, and she said if you aren't in your PJs in the next 60 seconds, I am going to lose my job. Oh please, oh *please* put your PJs on!" Perhaps a short period of begging is all it will take.

As mentioned in the discussion about Playlistening, you can even use a playful approach when providing discipline. Wrap the "no" in a silly accent or deliver the message from a funny character, and—voila!—you're setting limits. When my son got demanding about a ton of things he wanted in a catalog, I pretended to call him from the North Pole, impersonating an elf with a strange accent, and took down his holiday request list (yes, in September). He happily engaged in the game for a few minutes and then dropped his whiny routine. I didn't need to moralize or lecture about greed and ingratitude. I sidestepped all that and played a game he found fun. If you don't get an engaged response to a playful approach, your child may need the opportunity to express some strong feelings about the *no*, and that's OK too.

Play more! And learn new ways to play. There really can't be too much playing in one's home. It will make everyone feel better.

The good and bad wolf

Years ago, I read a fascinating book by Ann Hulbert called *Raising America: Experts, Parents, and a Century of Advice About Children.* In it, she shares research on child-rearing over the past hundred years and puts the various influences (from Freud to Spock to Brazelton) in the context of the newest research on child development. It covers a lot of ground over 350 pages, including strict versus permissive, child- versus parent-centered, and how the women's movement has affected parenting. But what struck me most was a query about the most basic of foundations upon which we each build our parenting approach. This was the question: *Do you believe that human beings are—at their core—inherently good...or not?* Your answer will significantly impact the way you interact with children.

Our beliefs about children guide how we think about and treat them. To bring us back to the beginning, many of our views on humanhood and parenting grow from seeds planted in *our* childhoods. This is why finding and reading your original parenting manual is so important. Sometimes we're not even aware of the beliefs we have or the stories we're telling ourselves. It reminds me of the hard to attribute quote: "Don't believe everything you think." It's counterintuitive to question yourself in this way, it's another paradox, but it brings clarity and insight if you do. It will ultimately help get you out of your head and into your body and, yes, *your heart.*

At the end of most of my parenting and staff development workshops, I tell the Cherokee legend of the two wolves. The story goes...

A grandfather sits with his young grandson, teaching him about the difference between good and bad, positive and negative, shadow and light.

"There is a good wolf and a bad wolf living inside each of us," the elder tells his grandchild, "The good wolf is love, compassion, courage, generosity, and every virtue of a human. The bad wolf is anger, hatred, laziness, greed, and other human vices. In each one of us, these two wolves are engaged in a fierce battle."

The grandson sits on the edge of his seat, hardly able to contain his anticipation.

"Which wolf will win?" he blurts out.

"The one you feed," his grandfather answers.

A child is a small human being and just like us, they are capable of both "good" and "bad" behavior. They have a shadow side. But they *will* learn to feed the right wolf. Set the best example you can, and then, be patient.

Isn't that what we are always telling them?

ACKNOWLEDGEMENTS

"Alone we can do so little; together we can do so much."
–Helen Keller

Books are like children; slowly forming within the dark recesses of the self. A spark is nurtured. Ideas take form on the page and then mature and grow. Just like real children, they need other caregivers—alloparents who help love and care for them. I am lucky to have had the "right number of adults" to support me in this endeavor.

Huge gratitude to my literary agency, Publishizer, especially my agent, Julia Guirado, who cold called me via LinkedIn messenger to ask if I wanted to write a second book. This project would never have been started without you. And thanks also to Lee Constantine for helping me negotiate my publisher pick. I am grateful to have had choices in that department and my hat is off to Steve Guidetti and the rest of the team at Isabella Media—thank you.

Thanks to my early readers without whom these pages would not exist: Karen Lane, your editing and encouraging of this book was vital to its completion. It was kismet that we found each other both online and in person. Your book is next. Thank you Mom (Kathi Pewitt), for your sharp eye and small edits. I know you love everything I write and so I appreciate when you find something to improve. Kelly Whelan, my soul-sister, you brought a unique lens to your edits and improved readability and accessibility so much. I can't wait to read your book. And thanks to your first-born, Ani, for their insight. Thank you Pasha Marlowe, rockstar goddess. You dove in and offered succinct and important feedback on a moment's notice. You are inspiring AF and I can't wait to read your book too!

To the women I can call in the middle of the night—I have no words for the deepness of love brought by decades of conflict, comfort, and connection. I love you and your families Bobbie Casey, Maria Casey, Dani Champlain, Daylen Jones, and Naomi Ryan.

I appreciate many more friends and family members: Juliet Gagnon and Team Shit-Chicken, the Grateful Eight (you know who you are), the Krakowskis, the Macutkiewicz family, the Endys, the Tozier-Schulzes, the MacLaughlin-de Brauws, the Goldstein-Lepps, the Hendricks family, the Brooklyn Goldsteins, the Perkins-Stenhouse family, the Kaufman-Beckensteins, the Floyds, the Meyerholz family, the Angells, all the Pewitts, the Goldstein-Squyres family, and the Collins and Kramer families. Knowing you, being supported by you, and raising kids alongside many of you is far better than I ever imagined.

A humble bow to my moms of boys group: The Future Mother-in-Law Society of Portland, Maine. I cannot measure the amount of support I've felt through the tears, fears, laughter, grief, joy, and support of the past 10 plus years. I love you Leah Deragon, Jen Everett, Stephanie Goss, Chiara Liberatore, Misty McLaughlin, Eliza Nichols, Shelley Walker Rosen, Tessy Seward, and Robin Tannenbaum.

I am grateful to Lisa Masure and Jennifer Boyden for reflecting on their empty nests and to Nancy Miller for the beautiful words about letting go. Thanks to everyone who has a story or quote about their family in this book, particularly Michelle Bourget, Alyson Spencer-Reed, and Adrianne Zahner.

Thanks to all my crowdfunding book buyers, every single one of you: friends, family members, and perfect strangers. Particular thanks to those who preordered three books or more and are not otherwise mentioned: Cecil Hodges, Charles Howes, Denise Castner, Emily Murray and staff at Birth Roots, Faye Joost, Irene Di Minervino, Jennifer Giaramita, Jeannie Riedel, Jodi Phinney, Kirsten Cyr, Lisa Lalumiere at Little Red

Caboose Child Development Center, Maya Coleman, Meg Harpool at River School House, Meghan Jones, Melissa Hamlin, Nola Fennessy, Rana O'Connor and everyone on the Southern Maine Foster Family Recruitment Team, Sara Hicks-Kilday, and Resa Jones and crew at the Children's Nursery School.

As is said, I stand on the tall shoulders of many giants in the parenting education, early childhood, and self-development fields. Too many to name them all, though some are mentioned throughout this book. Thank you Pam Leo, grandmother of connection parenting. I think about how I first discovered you through an online search and am still floored that we've become friends. You wrote a beautiful foreword and I'm so glad you know me as a person and parent. Thank you Patty Wiplfer for reviewing my words about the five Listening Tools and to my many talented colleagues at Hand in Hand Parenting (I'm looking at you, Karen Wolfe!). My coworkers at ZERO TO THREE and HealthySteps are the best—a brilliant and committed team focused on the vital goal of ensuring all babies and toddlers have a strong start in life. When I landed my job as a writer there, I told my then eight-year-old that it would be like him getting a job where he gets to play with LEGO® all day—lucky me!

Last, but far from least, I remember the day I asked my family how they felt about me writing another book and got two enthusiastic thumbs-up. They surely were not thinking about the times leading up to a deadline where I would stay up late and then be crabby the next day. Thank you for your patience. I love you Rich MacLaughlin, it's been a wild ride and I'm beyond thrilled you've been sitting beside me all these years. *We. Will. Prevail.* And finally, this one's for you, Josh MacLaughlin—my favorite child and best teacher. You give me reason to stay clear in my convictions about childhood and parenting—thank you for letting me share your stories here. I love you **more** and know you'll grow up with a strong, deep, and loving heart.

CPSIA information can be obtained
at www.ICGtesting.com
Printed in the USA
JSHW022311040521
14317JS00006B/40